# THE ART OF
# COUNSELING

# THE ART OF COUNSELING

## by Rollo May

INTRODUCTION BY HARRY BONE

ABINGDON
Nashville

THE ART OF COUNSELING

*ISBN 0-687-01765-3*

MANUFACTURED BY THE PARTHENON PRESS AT
NASHVILLE, TENNESSEE, UNITED STATES OF AMERICA

# TO

BOB AND ROGER AND LEE AND GALEN

*and others of my counselees whose per-
sonalities cross and re-cross the pages of
this book*

*Foreword*

THIS BOOK is an exploration of a new field. During late years counseling has become increasingly important. Not only the dean who must deal with the brilliant student who is flunking, or the student director who is appealed to by the timid freshman oppressed by an inferiority feeling, but the minister calling in the home, the camp director with his youngsters by the lakeside, the teacher with sixth-graders or college seniors—in short, an infinite number of persons in innumerable vocations are realizing that they are called upon to do counseling, to mold personality, whether they wish it or not. "Guide, counselor, and friend"—that is what we all are whenever we deal intimately with people, which may be a hundred times a day.

Out of this new importance of counseling has arisen the need, expressed particularly among leaders in student work, for a book in this field. Counseling is an art, yes, but an art which can be peculiarly stimulated and developed, even more than one's painting and music. For people are the medium in which we all work.

In the following pages is utilized the new understanding of personality offered by the modern authorities in the field, the psychotherapists Freud, Jung, Rank, and Kunkel. Particularly does this discussion owe a debt to the humble and penetrating wisdom of Alfred Adler, with whom I have had the privilege of studying, associating, and discussing intimately. In counseling one does not, of course, use the technique of the psychotherapists as such; but one can well profit from their discoveries in one's own adventure in the understanding of people.

This material is a development from lectures originally given at the seminars of student workers on "Counseling and Personality Adjustment" of the Methodist Episcopal Church, South, in North Carolina and Arkansas in the summers of 1937 and 1938. To the members of those seminars, for all their kindness and help as we explored together this field, and especially to Dr. W. M. Alexander and Mr. Boyd McKeown, I express gratitude. I have retained the more direct and personal approach of the seminar, and I hope the citing of examples from my own experience will be pardoned as an endeavor to make the material more living and useful for other counselors.

It is my hope that this book will give to the reader, in addition to assistance in the technique of counseling, aid in the understanding of his own personality problems. Particularly the first and third sections are planned to assist the reader in adjusting his own personality for his most creative work and happiest expression in the outside world.

Because of the newness of the field of counseling, our conclusions should be regarded as tentative, pointing toward that time when, through a pooling of experience and knowledge, we shall be able to take advantage of the best contributions of psychotherapy for religious and educational work.

Dr. Harry Bone has given indispensable aid in the preparation of this manuscript. And may I also express deep gratitude to Professor Paul Tillich, whose comprehensive learning and affectionate insight into human nature have lent me something of their wealth; and to Dean Henry

## FOREWORD

Pitney VanDusen, Dr. Victor Obenhaus, Dr. David Roberts, and Dr. E. McLung Fleming for reading and making suggestions on parts of the manuscript. Florence DeFrees May has given help at every point, and even more valuably, has taught me what great creative potentialities love can release in personality.

ROLLO MAY

*Verona, New Jersey.*

*Acknowledgments*

THE AUTHOR and the publishers are grateful to the various publishers and holders of copyrights for kind permission to use various quotations in this book. A complete bibliography of books quoted or referred to will be found on page 243. Special acknowledgment is due the following publishers:

George Allen and Unwin, Limited, publishers of *How Natives Think*, by Lucien Levy-Bruhl, translated by Lillian A. Clare.

Greenberg, Publisher, publisher of *Understanding Human Nature*, by Alfred Adler, translated by Walter Beran Wolfe.

Harcourt, Brace and Company, publishers of *Modern Man in Search of a Soul*, by C. G. Jung, translated by W. S. Dell and C. F. Baynes; and of *Psychological Types*, by C. G. Jung, translated by H. Godwin Baynes.

Alfred A. Knopf, Incorporated, publishers of *Truth and Reality* and *Will Therapy*, by Otto Rank, translated by Jessie Taft.

Yale University Press, publishers of *Psychology and Religion*, by C. G. Jung.

# Contents

## Part 2

## PRACTICAL STEPS

## Part 3

## ULTIMATE CONSIDERATIONS

# CONTENTS

*Introduction*

## THE FIELD OF COUNSELING

DEVELOPMENTS in various fields in recent years have resulted in the emergence of a rather special type of endeavor which has come to be called counseling. The practice of helping by advice, counsel, guidance, sympathy, and encouragement, both informally (friend to friend) and professionally (priest to communicant, doctor to patient, teacher to pupil), is immemorial. The essence of the contemporary practice of counseling lies in an attempt to make the act of helping more effective by basing it on such knowledge of human character, its making, unmaking, and re-making, as can be contributed by the various branches of contemporary psychology. That there is a special province for the counselor—who is properly equipped by temperament and training—is indicated by the urgent need of many people today for a kind of help which is not provided by the well known specialties. To put it concretely: If one is physically ill one needs a medical doctor; if one is ill with an illness or personality maladjustment that arises from both physical and mental causes one needs a psychiatrist (a medical doctor who specializes in nervous disorders and is also trained in psychotherapy); if one suffers from personality problems which are psychological and not due to any physical cause, a consulting psychologist or "lay" (nonmedical) psychotherapist is indicated; in as far as one is immature or uninstructed one needs schooling, an educator.

The field of the counselor lies between those of the last two professions mentioned, and the counselor shares part of the equipment of each. The educator (secular or religious) deals with "normal" individuals and is concerned with the processes of growth and development—intellectual, moral, or religious. The consulting psychologist deals chiefly with corrective or re-educational problems in individuals who have become involved in serious difficulties of adjustment and who often require extended individual treatment. However, no categorical distinction can be made between the needs of individuals for "education" and for "re-education," respectively. Remedial and disciplinary problems are a "statistically normal" part of the educator's routine, and the consulting psychologist makes more or less use of positive educational procedures according to the requirements of a given situation. The counselor deals with problems which are too complicated to be solved incidentally in the ordinary course of educational procedure, but not so serious as to require the particular specialized services of a consulting psychologist. (As a matter of fact, there are many types of problems which might be handled by either a counselor or a consulting psychologist; in these cases the relative unavailability of the latter, for financial or geographical reasons, enhances the need for qualified counselors.)

Counseling is less a profession than a technique or art which is to be employed as part of a more inclusive responsibility in those professions whose chief business is with persons; namely, in the work of doctors, teachers, principals, deans, pastors, religious workers, and social workers. ("Psychiatric social work" is a branch of the latter profession that has established courses and standards of training in the science and art of helping persons which, it is hoped,

will soon be taken seriously by the other professions listed.)
Naturally the possibilities of doing counseling in any of
these professions depends upon the time available, the in-
clination, and the personality and information equipment
of the individual.

The present book is one of the few but growing number of those which are exploring an area of fundamental
importance, the interrelation of Christianity and mental
hygiene, and should be of value both to those who have
and to those who have not taken courses of training in
counseling. The author, who is well equipped for his task
by his personal qualifications and his training and experience
in the several fields pertinent to the discussions, is to be
commended especially for certain features of his work.
He has rightly neglected the specialized psychotherapeutic
techniques which cannot be utilized by the counselor, but
has drawn freely and discriminatingly from the various
"schools" a number of conceptions which are of great
value and fully applicable in counseling. He has kept close
to his actual experience; and while this procedure sacrifices
something in scope, it makes for sincerity and vital con-
creteness. Finally, he presents a number of ideas on the
relation—theoretical and practical—of religion and psychology which are original and stimulating.

HARRY BONE, *Consulting Psychologist*

*New York City*

# PART ONE
# UNDERLYING PRINCIPLES

*"The unexamined life is not worth living."*
SOCRATES

*"I saw that all the things I feared had nothing good or bad in them save as the mind was affected by them."*
*"He who understands himself and his emotions loves God, and the more so the more he understands himself and his emotions."*
SPINOZA

*"A thing that is explained ceases to concern us. What did the God mean who gave the advice, 'Know thyself!' to Socrates? Did it perhaps imply: 'Cease to be concerned about thyself! become objective!'?"*
NIETZSCHE

*Chapter I*

## THE SOURCE OF PERSONALITY PROBLEMS

### CASE OF GEORGE B.

GEORGE B. made an excellent impression upon me when he came into my office. He must have been over six feet in height, and his physique was unusually well-proportioned and handsome. He shook my hand warmly, though a little too violently, and looked at me fixedly as he spoke in a slow, carefully controlled voice.

His problem was a general unhappiness in college life. This was surprising, for to all superficial appearances George was the type which fits into campus life with eminent success. Now a sophomore, he was considering dropping out of college altogether. Concentration on his studies had become increasingly difficult for him during the past weeks, and a general nervousness had come upon him for some reason he could not understand. He had shifted his course from physical education to liberal arts, but this had not helped. The reason for this shift, George said, was the low morale of the faculty of the former department; he mentioned with particular disgust the coach's drinking beer on one of the trips of the minor team to which he belonged. In fact George condemned the whole faculty, and he had written a paper to prove their inadequacy.

As counselor I permitted him, of course, to continue talking. He proceeded to explain to me his dissatisfaction also with the religious work on the campus; it lacked "punch," to use his term. He expressed a desire to get into the student religious work and reform it—and at this moment his voice, which had previously been calm and controlled, quivered with emotion. He was, it became evident, a very religious individual in the ordinary sense of the term.

I inquired about his friendships—an area which is always significant in personality maladjustments. George answered that he felt lonely on the campus. He did not like his roommate, a freshman who irritated him in all sorts of small ways, such as taking a long time getting ready for bed. George vowed he would get him over this vexatious habit if he had to punch him every night! In the area of relationships with the opposite sex, it came out that George was then dating one of the more attractive and popular girls on the campus; but he felt that she was too frivolous and needed to be reformed into taking a greater interest in serious things. One of the highest rating social fraternities had given him a bid to membership, a matter which he was considering at the time of these interviews. His scholastic average in college was only mediocre, although, he claimed, he forced himself to study very hard.

This young man was clearly approaching a crisis in his personality development. During that very month his condition was growing worse. The tensions within his personality were becoming so great and troublesome that concentration on his studies was almost impossible, and he was finding difficulty in sleeping at night. His moods changed violently from exaltation—during which periods he greeted me with an indomitable smile and assured me buoyantly, "I'm on top of the world today!"—to deep depression, when I sometimes observed him wandering around the campus in a sort of daze. His physical condition became so poor that he was advised by college health officials to drop out of school for a complete rest.

Here we have a condition which verges on what is commonly termed a "nervous breakdown." Many of the items cited in the above description of George's case sound like trifles, but they are symptomatic of something more serious occurring underneath. He could have become definitely neurotic if he had kept on in the path we see him pursuing; the embryonic form of neurosis, indeed, is observable in this bare outline.

How shall we deal with such personality difficulties? This general condition is not at all infrequently found on college campuses, it will be admitted, or in any groups of young people, or even adults for that matter. Shall we send George home for a rest? This would accomplish no permanent good. When he returned to some field of active life the journey toward neurosis would be begun all over again, for the real causes in the form of unresolved personality tensions would still be present. Should the counselor endeavor calmly to reason the matter out, trying to persuade George that the college is not as bad as he thinks and that everything can't be altogether out-of-joint? This would lead to an argument the result of which would only be to re-enforce George's prejudices. No, the counselor must take the deeper approach of psychological understanding if he is to help in such a case.

In endeavoring to understand George's personality pattern—and this is where the source of his difficulties is to be found—I learned that he was the second child following a daughter in a farming family in which considerable emphasis had been placed upon religious and ethical matters. His sister had attended this college before him and had set a fairly high record in campus achievement.

The outstanding feature observable in George's personality is his tremendous ambition. This takes the form of a strong drive to dominate others, such as his roommate, his girl, and in fact even the college faculty. This ambition is understandable partly in connection with his excellent physique, which must have lent him much prestige in his pre-college years. It is also partly understandable (but here we must go cautiously) in his relation to his older sister; second children often manifest an exaggerated ambition because of their early striving to keep up with or overtake the older child. This is particularly true of a boy following a girl, for the girl develops more rapidly in the early years.

An exaggerated ambition such as in George's drive to dominate others is often connected fundamentally with an inferiority feeling. The individual feels himself deeply inferior, and therefore he strives to make himself superior by endeavoring to reform others and forcing them to conform to his standards. There are clear indications of George's having a strong inferiority feeling. We should expect him to express his urge to surpass others on the college athletic field, for physical education has been his main interest; but he has not succeeded in making any of the major college teams. He does not blame the coaches outright for this failure—the psychological processes are more subtle than that; he shifts the contest to the moral realm and proceeds to criticize the coaches for their beer drinking.

This personality, unusually ambitious to begin with, demands much prestige but does not succeed in achieving it in the usual channels. But it can achieve it in the moral area, and so George proceeds to center his attention upon the faults of people around him. He criticizes the college faculty and sets out to reform everything from his girl to the campus religious program. This is his way of "putting his ego on top," as Adler would say. George is very religious; but he is using his religion, as it is not uncommonly used, as an ego-weapon rather than as a cause for unselfish devotion. Temporarily this little strategy succeeds; there is no denying that in his reforming zeal, George's ego ascends on its own scale of prestige. But the victory is poorly won. For his little successes in dominating will make him more antisocial, separate him the more from his group (such as his fellow students, the coaches, and his girl). And so what remnants of genuine prestige he now enjoys will steadily diminish; his inferiority feeling and basic insecurity will increase; he will need to strive the more desperately to dominate others; and his whole problem will steadily become worse.

This is the vicious circle in which persons with severe personality problems become caught. No wonder George feels nervously tense and cannot sleep or concentrate! No wonder he must exert the special control over himself manifested in his slow actions and his very steady, self-conscious manner of speaking. The tension within his personality between inferiority feeling and exaggerated ambition will of course make impossible for him any happy and creative living.

It is such internal tensions that cause nervous breakdowns, not simply overwork. George is caught in the vicious circle of egocentric ambition, and his personality difficulty will become steadily worse—unless a "clarification," a clearing up of wrong attitudes, occurs—until he breaks in definite neurosis. For his girl, we can predict, will throw him over; to the extent that she has a normal and wholesome attitude toward life she will not brook his reforming tendencies. We can also predict that he will not join the fraternity, for to do so would be to surrender the privilege of dominating people around him.

In our counseling periods I gradually pointed out to George these aspects of his personality pattern. At first he could not understand his selfish ambition or his urge to dominate others; he insisted he "loved" all people, and wished to reform them for their own good. We cannot expect such an individual, incidentally, to understand immediately the egocentric nature of his little strategies; for if he did understand he would have to give up his egocentricity, and that is the last thing in the world he wishes to do.

But in the meantime he was suffering; and through relating these sufferings to the mistakes in his personality pattern, we were able to turn the vicious circle of his battle for false prestige into a constructive circle. He then began to find socially constructive means of expression for his ambition. He became a member of the campus Christian Association cabinet, but his zeal to change everything at first made it difficult for the other students to work with him. Having rejected the invitation to join the fraternity he threw himself into a project for investigating and reforming the fraternities!—this was his way of making contact with them without joining. He then organized a house group of his own, but threatened to back out at the last minute when he did not get his way in the choice of a house.

As he began to get social recognition for constructive accomplishments, however, he was gradually relieved of the intense pressure of his inferiority feeling. And consequently he did not feel so compelled to dominate. Once started on the constructive circle, George began to develop into as positive and helpful a force in his community as he had previously been negative. Without going into the details in his personality change, may we point out that it was not, of course, a simple and easy matter. The readjustment of tensions within his personality—what we term clarification—was not accomplished over night or even in a couple of months. And the readjustment brought with it its pain, the throes of re-birth from egocentricity to the socially constructive attitude toward life. But nature throws its assisting forces behind the individual once he has begun the constructive circle; there is a geometric progression in the respect that the more healthy the personality becomes the more it is enabled to obtain new health. This was so for George. As soon as he gave the campus a chance it quickly recognized his creative abilities, his physical attractiveness, and his unusual energies. The very powers which had led him to the brink of neurosis now worked to increase his genuine leadership and prestige. The relationship with his girl could not be salvaged; she broke off with him, but although he suffered greatly he did not slip back into his old moralistic isolation.

In the spring of the year he was elected president of the college Christian Association, a position at which he worked hard but still unsteadily and temperamently. But by the next year his efforts had grown so socially constructive that he became prominent in the Men's League and was eventually elected to the Student Council as one of the outstanding student leaders on the campus.

### CREATIVE TENSIONS

WHAT, then, is the source of personality difficulties? If George B. in this case had been sent home in a state of nervous collapse, people would have blamed his trouble on "overwork." But we have observed through our psychological understanding of George's personality that the real reason for his breakdown would not have been too much work, but rather unadjusted tensions within his personality. The old custom of explaining nervous breakdowns

27

with an apologetic, "He carries so much responsibility," or, "He tries to do too much," with the conclusion that all the individual needs is a good rest, is in most cases false. The more pertinent question is, why does he take on too much work? What tensions are there within his personality which will not permit him to carry the work which he has assumed? It is evident that persons often throw themselves into a great bulk of work as an escape from unsolved personality problems.

The source of personality problems is a *lack of adjustment of tensions within the personality*. In George's case we observed a too egocentric ambition (manifesting itself in his striving to dominate) on one hand, and a too weak social interest (evidencing itself in a failure to co-operate with others) on the other. The more unbalanced these tensions became in George's personality, the closer he would come to a nervous breakdown; the greater this lack of adjustment, in other words, the more neurotic he would grow. Only when the tensions were adjusted into some kind of functional accord would George be able to express himself creatively and effectively in the outside world and thus achieve the genuine prestige which he craved.

Each of us has experienced this process of adjustment of tensions within his own personality. It is something dynamic, creative, going on at all times. A man walks down the street, for example; and in talking to the first person he accosts he experiences a re-adjusting of the tensions between his desire to dominate and his interest in the other as a fellow human being. Or he comes home and reads a book, and every idea that catches his attention sets his personality tensions into a new adjustment. Every time one experiences a feeling that one "ought" to do this or that, or a feeling of inferiority, or of triumph or despair, one's personality tensions are being re-adjusted.

Thus personality is never static. It is alive, ever-changing, mobile; it is plastic, variable, almost protean. We should not therefore speak of "balance" in personality, or "equilibrium," for these imply that one's personality tensions can be set once for all. Becoming static is in this realm synonymous with death. Life is not like tuning a radio set and leaving it there; it is rather like continually tuning it to a varying wave-length, namely, the new experiences of each day which, flowing out of the infinite creativity of life, are always fresh and different.

At the same time this does not mean that one is an altogether different person from what one was yesterday, or that the individual is blown hither and yon like a wisp in the wind. There is a certain continuity because of the tendencies in the unconsciousness of the individual which reach deep down into his past experience. What he was a month ago, or a year or five or many years ago, leaves a certain psychic force within his unconsciousness which affects his tensions today. But these tendencies surging up from unconsciousness are also mobile and dynamic; one has an infinite number of them available at any given instance. That is why even habits cannot be static. It is doubtful whether there is any such thing as a real habit in healthy living, for there is no situation that does not bring in a new element of experience which affects the tensions within one's personality. Life is much more creative, much more variable and pregnant with possibilities than most people realize.

We use the world "tension" advisedly. For there is always a certain stretching, even a stress and strain in one's personality. There is a pull, for example, between where one is now and where one must be in an hour, and this awareness of obligation to be some other place exerts a certain tension in the mind. There is a tension between the work one did yesterday and the work one is to do to-morrow, and one carries this strain along from day to day as though bearing the burden of labor upon one's back. The great tension, of course, is that which we speak of broadly as the tension between what one is and what one feels one ought to be. Personality is like a web, to venture a very imperfect simile; for it consists of lines of tension between an infinitely larger number of points, the tensions and the points of attachment being continually subject to change.

It is a serious mistake, therefore, to speak of personality without tensions—to imply, for example, that the healthy mental condition is a blissful absence of tensions. To be sure, tensions which are seriously maladjusted and are therefore stretched to the breaking point do result in mental breakdown. But the thing desired is *adjustment* of tensions, not escaping of them. One could not get rid of personality tensions even if one wanted to; the neurotic attempts it, by such schemes, for example, as remaining indoors and never meeting other people; but the result is stagnation and ultimate breakdown. One must coura-geously accept the necessity for tensions and then work out the most effective adjustment so that one's personality will express itself most creatively in the outside world.

The point deserves emphasis that the locus of the personality problem is the adjustment of tensions *within* the individual. Outside factors play a role, of course; but their importance lies in the fact that the personality draws them into itself and uses them as pivot points. The talk about the need for "adjustment to environment" which was so common among the dilettantes of the new psychology several years ago, implying that a person's main concern should be making himself over to fit his environment, falsifies the problem and belittles human personality. As though a man were a piece of rubber useful only because it can be stretched to fit anything! Yes, adjustment is necessary, but not merely to something outside the individual. It is a creative, dynamic, primarily inner process.

The counselor should guard against the counselee's tendency to shift his problem to some area outside himself, blaming, for example, someone in his environment. It was a wise young lady who once came to me with the statement, "I can't get along with my family; tell me what is wrong with me." It is most fruitful for the counselor, though taking duly into consideration all environmental factors, to push the difficulty back to the tensions *within* the personality of the counselee.

Even so apparently objective a factor as sex expression becomes important to personality because of the inward tensions it sets up. If it were only a question of man's expressing his sex urge in reality, expression equalling mental health and non-expression equalling neurosis, what a simple problem it would be! But sex causes personality difficulties, as Freud rightly points out, not to the extent that it is objectively expressed in reality, but according to how the individual takes this expression or lack of it. One of my counselees had previously gone to a professor to talk over his problem of general unhappiness and melancholy, and had been advised by the professor to go out and express himself sexually. The student experimented in the field but found that it made his difficulty all the worse. Libertinism and all other attempts to work out the problem entirely *outside one's self* can make the individual just as neurotic as ascetic repression. Freud makes it clear that the problem of sex is one of the adjusting of tensions within the personality—the tension of the sex urge, the social requirements as they appear to the individual, and the influence of moral training, all forming a none too simple situation. What is desired is a clarification of attitudes, which Freud seeks through psychoanalysis; and right behavior results from this.

Something outside the individual is used, generally, as an occasion for the personality breakdown, such as a love affair, or a severe examination, or the death of a member of the family. Here is John Doe, let us say, who commits suicide when his sweatheart throws him over. People say, "If only he had never met the woman, this would not have happened." Possibly—but probably not. For he carried neurotic behavior potentially within himself, and it would have come out in some form sooner or later. The significant area in regard to these tensions is within the personality, although the individual will be continually acting and reacting in his environment, using elements in it as pivotal points. George B., we remember, was angry at his roommate; but the roommate in the case was merely the most convenient pivotal point for his irritability; and we can be sure if the roommate had not been around George would have used the maid or somebody else as a butt for his irritability. The personality uses the points in the environment as nails on which to attach the end threads of tension. Thus these outside elements become important because they are related to the personality tensions within. The personality, we may say, takes these elements of the environment into itself and uses them in its own structure.

The tendency to blame heredity or environment for personality difficulties should be avoided. The unattractive girl may say, "Well, I just wasn't born beautiful"; but the counselor can often indicate to her that her unattractiveness is due to mistaken attitudes and therefore wrong use of the physical form with which she was born. Neuroses—the general classification of personality difficulties when they become severe—are not inherited but are wrong ways of using what one inherits.

Environment is extremely important as the arena in which the individual struggles for his adjustment, but to regard environment as causal is neither fruitful nor accurate. Environment furnishes the chessboard and in fact most of the pawns with which the game is played; given the board and pawns, however, one cannot predict *how* the game will be played.

It is not within the scope of this book to delve into the very important question of the bearing of social conditions upon the individual's personality problems. Such diseases of society as unemployment, economic insecurity of all sorts, fear of war and the social upheaval that follows war have a tremendous bearing upon the adjustment of individuals concerned. Spasmodic unemployment with its consequent continuous burden of insecurity increases the personality tensions with a severity the importance of which cannot be exaggerated. It is a truism to say that mental health and a healthy social order are intimately interdependent.

Granting all this and more, it is still true, however, that the personality difficulty itself is a matter of adjustment of tensions within the individual; and the endeavor to locate it outside is to miss the point of the matter. To be sure, unfavorable environments such as that of the child growing up in the slums make personality problems more likely. But it is a commonplace that two children growing up in poverty-stricken conditions may develop very differently. In fact, two children in the same home, thus beginning with almost identical heredity and almost identical environment not only may, but as we discover, *will* develop into appreciably different types of personality. Heredity and environment set limits within which the individual does his developing; he who comes from a line of short ancestors need not expect to grow extraordinarily tall—but his physical health does not depend upon how tall he is. Personality health is a *qualitative* not a quantitative matter.

The mere changing of environment, although sometimes helpful, is not the essential need. A daughter away at college, for example, gets mixed up in an unfortunate love affair, and the parents remove her to another school. This may help temporarily, but the probability is that the girl will get into similar difficulties again unless some better adjustment of her personality has occurred in the meantime. "They change their skies but not their minds, who fly across the seas," and personality problems are a question of changing one's mind.

As counselors we sometimes seek to effect a change in certain features of the environments of our counselees, particularly if they be children. In counseling with adults the counselor will not suggest outright a change in the environment even though it appear advisable; he will rather aid the individual to understand himself in relation to the environment, and then the decision to change will come from the counselee himself. The changing of the vocational factor in the environment often comes into the picture: a person of a peculiarly artistic temperament will occasionally be caught in an occupation which makes the overcoming of his neurosis almost humanly impossible. It is within the counselor's province to assist individuals to discover their right vocations; but this kind of guidance, it should be remembered, is one degree removed from direct dealing with personality problems. Even beyond this there will be the times when the counselor gives the individual specific help in finding a job; to one burdened with economic insecurity practical aid is at the moment more important than psychological understanding. But in these instances the counselor, strictly speaking, is dealing only indirectly with personality difficulties. When he deals with the personality problem itself, he does not permit the counselee to shift the responsibility to the environment, but aids the counselee to accept responsibility himself for his future and helps him to use his environment in the most creative way.

A girl once came to me for counseling who had lived through the most unfavorable of environments. She had grown up in a stepmother's house with two stepaunts, a stepbrother and several other in-laws and grandparents, who had crowded her even out of her own bed. There had been continual quarreling in the house; and the adults naturally picked her, the stepchild, as a convenient butt for the expression of their rancor. He who thinks that environment makes the person would expect this girl to be, after fifteen years of family torment, a cynical, suspicious, scheming misanthrope. But, as a matter of fact she was an attractive, socially minded young woman, possessing more humor and gaiety than the other girls of her set. She had met her unhappy situation by developing a more than usual amount of humor and buoyancy. We could cite many similar cases where the individual has used an unfavorable environment as a ladder to climb to an unusually effective personality adjustment. Bad environment increases the possibility of neurosis, but the individual may use this very potentiality for a more creative adjustment to living. To assist in the accomplishment of this latter is the function of the counselor.

### STRUCTURE OF DIFFICULTIES

LET US now get more clearly in mind the structure of personality difficulties. The lack of adjustment of tensions within the personality may manifest itself in all sorts of symptoms, such as embarrassment, timidity, extraordinary shyness, continuous worry and anxiety, fears of meeting people, special fear of failure in one's job, and inability to concentrate. Embarrassment, for example, is a sign that the tensions within the personality block each other, like two wrestlers who have such strong holds on each other that neither can move. Consequently the individual cannot speak or think freely and cannot express himself effectively in the outside world. Individuals who are not able adequately to adjust the tensions within their personalities may consequently be severely handicapped in the execution of their work, or be unable to make normal social contacts and thus solve their love and marriage problems or in other ways fail to develop and utilize their potentialities.

The individual with such a personality difficulty has a conflict within himself which to some extent paralyzes him. He is, as the expression goes, at odds with himself. Because he is at odds with himself, he is also at odds with his social group. The two are conflicts on two flanks of the same battle. George B. could not get along with the other students because he insisted on reforming them, but this was in turn connected with his inner drive to dominate. Attaining mental health meant in his case, as it does in all cases, a simultaneous adjustment of the tensions within himself and the adjustment of his relations with his fellows. Adler makes the social adjustment the criterion, the "fruits," by which the personality clarification is judged. But this runs the danger of glorifying superficial adjustment to society. Actually behavior toward others results from attitudes; and there is only one seat of attitudes, namely the mind of the individual in question. The person who has made his adjustment to society without clarification of his attitudes, that is, at the price of hypocrisy, has made no adjustment at all, and his little structure will collapse erelong. Likewise, it is possible for an individual, such as a Socrates or a St. Francis, to have attained a creative adjustment of his inner personality tensions and be for that very reason out of harmony with the imperfect society of a particular period.

When a personality problem becomes so severe that the individual cannot carry on in his work or his relations with other people, we describe it by the term "neurosis." A student, for example, had the relatively common problem of studying at a high nervous tension before examinations. This grew more severe until he became sick the night before an examination and was excused; and he then developed the convenient neurotic scheme of falling sick before *all* examinations. A similar neurotic condition may be brought on by a severe emotional conflict which cannot be resolved by the individual.

The term "neurosis" springs from the root word "nerves," because mental disorders were first observed through the nervousness which they generated in the form of anxiety, worry, or even actual trembling of parts of the body. But the term does not imply that anything is wrong with the nerves organically; it refers, rather, to a personality state. "Psychosis" is the term for that state of mental disorder more severe than neurosis, which includes those many forms of mental disease popularly lumped as insanity. Some psychoses are organic, such as those caused by disease attacking the tissues of the nervous system; but many are functional. It is outside the sphere of this book to discuss psychoses. The counselor does not, of course, attempt to deal with such conditions, and the particular value in being able to recognize psychotic conditions is that he can refer the individual to professional psychiatric care.

Neuroses are functional in root, due, that is, to forms of behavior and mental attitudes rather than organic disorders. There may be concomitant organic factors; an organ inferiority, as Adler has demonstrated, may be a casual factor in a neurosis. Many organic states are results of neurotic states of mind, such as low blood pressure or, to cite the classical illustration, blindness coming with shellshock during wars. The counselor should be aware of the physical condition of his counselee so as to bring into the picture all the relevant organic factors, either causal or resultant. He can often get aid in this through consultation with the family doctor of the counselee, or the college health officials in campus situations. The counselor concerns himself with the functional aspect of the difficulty, namely, the making healthy of the attitudes and behavior patterns of the individual.

It is generally recognized in modern psychotherapy that there is no hard and fast line between so-called "normal" people and neurotics, nor between neurotics and psychotics. Many types of psychotics are required by law to be confined to institutions for the insane; but psychiatrists and judges admit that the decision as to whom to adjudge insane and whom to dismiss as merely "a little off" is at times unavoidably arbitrary. It is possible for an individual to progress from a simple personality problem to neurosis and from neurosis to psychosis, and then back again. One could cite many cases similar to that of Mrs. D. who had had personality difficulties in her youth but had moved with a fair degree of success through grade school and high school. Her personality conflicts became more pronounced in college, and we should then have classified her as neurotic. Several years later, in the course of an emotional and physical strain, she suddenly developed a case of schizophrenia ("split personality") and was confined to a mental hospital. She is now out of the hospital living in fairly healthy fashion, and is to all appearances as "normal" as people around her.

Everyone has personality problems, and everyone is continuously in the process of re-adjusting the tensions within his personality. No one is completely "normal." For example, we all have had the wish at some time not to meet a certain other person; we may have crossed the street, though we were probably ashamed of it afterwards, to avoid encountering this person. Now if this grows into a desire to avoid a number of persons, or possibly everybody, so that we remain always behind closed doors at home, we shall have regressed into the neurotic state. In each of us there is the urge to dominate that drove George B. to the brink of neurosis. The difference is that those of us who are called "normal" have this tendency better adjusted in the constellation of our personality tensions. To speak frankly, I have never dealt with a counselee in whose difficulty I did not see myself, at least potentially. Every counselor, theoretically, will have this same experience. It is a matter of "There, but for the grace of God, go I." There is no room for arrogance or self-righteousness, but all the room in the world for humility, in the counseling occupation.

It is only wise for each of us to get acquainted with his little neurotic tendencies, even if they be no more severe than the common practice of running other people down in gossip or taking a drink of liquor to brace one's self for an important occasion. As Adler puts it, "Minor difficulties equal normality; major difficulties equal neurosis." Or, phrased probably more accurately, emotional conflicts which can be managed equal normality; those conflicts which the individual cannot manage equal neurosis.

If one recognizes one's special neurotic tendencies, one is more able to guard against their throwing the personality into definite disorder at some time of emotional crisis.

We have used the word "normal" in quotation marks, for it is an ideal rather than a reality. The norm is a standard drawn from our knowledge of the possibilities in a situation; it is partly based upon the range of expectation, but like physical health it is not a limiting category. It is possible to measure what is wrong or unhealthy in personality, for the neurosis leads the sick person into all kinds of errors, but we cannot measure "rightness" in this area. We can only free the individual to develop according to his own unique form. Thus being normal does not at all mean becoming static or "average" or fitted into the same pigeon-hole with everyone else; it means just the opposite of this. The norm for personality is in a sense the ideal; and it is based upon principles of creativity, such as freedom, individuality, and others which shall be discussed in the next chapter.

The possibility of re-adjusting personality tensions is nature's greatest gift to man. For it means growth, development, fulfilling of one's potentialities. Readjustment of personality tensions is synonymous with creativity. The especially creative person is precisely he whose personality tensions are especially susceptible to adjustment; he is more sensitive and suffers more, but he enjoys greater possibilities. The neurotic individual is one who has the special possibility of readjusting his personality tensions, who is required by the situation, in fact, to do so, but who because of his fear refuses and attempts to freeze himself into static training formulae. Once he takes courage and begins the process of readjustment, he may suddenly become an unusually creative individual. It is not an accident that the persons who are most sensitive to others, who may dread most meeting other people, are often precisely those who, when they turn this sensitivity into constructive channels, become most likable and effective in personal relationships.

One has only to glance through history to see that the most creative individuals are often the most obviously neurotic in tendency. Van Gogh was neurotic during most of his life and held off psychosis only by means of his tremendous creativity, by which he was able to effect a precarious adjustment of the terrific tensions in his personality. He existed on the thin, knife-blade edge of sanity only with difficulty; and this is connected with the creativity that made him a great artist. The great artists have a greater neurotic potentiality. They appear like Dostoevski and Nietzsche to fluctuate between more and less neurotic conditions. The more sensitive the inward balance of tensions, the greater the creativity. This is not to glorify neurosis; nor is it to say, with the title of a modern book, "be glad you're neurotic"; but it is to say that neurotic tendencies, if confronted courageously and constructively, do mean possibilities for special creative development.

Each of us, then, can achieve a better adjustment of his personality tensions. No man has "arrived." The difference between the neurotic who can barely keep his job and the "average" individual who does his work passably well is certainly no greater than that between this average person and the one who has become so clarified in his personality that he is able to take advantage of his creative possibilities and move rapidly up to increasingly influential and effective positions.

The helping of these so-called "normal" people to a more creative adjustment is an important aspect of the work of the counselor. He not only helps individuals below the average to come up to it; even more importantly, he aims to

41

assist those who appear to be average to take advantage of their unique possibilities and grow up in richer development. The following case may illustrate this.

When this young man, whom we may term John C., came to college, he passed as a typical freshman, possibly a little above average. During his freshman year he appeared more than usually shy; he blushed often and sat in committee meetings stiffly and soberly.

In his sophomore year he came to me with the request for a "phychological analysis." Though the process of counseling should scarcely be called that, we did arrange for a series of consultations. In the course of the counseling it came out that he had been brought up by a grandmother, and though he had been rather successful in his small high school as student council member and editor of the annual, he had always lived in rather solitary fashion. He could not remember playing much as a child, but he did remember mowing the lawn regularly and doing his little duties by himself. He was even then writing poems to "death." John C., evidently, was the type we customarily term "introvert." He had no satisfactory friendships with girls because of his shyness, which took the form of pronounced soberness when he was in social groups. He was distinctly intelligent, although his thought and speech moved slowly; his main interests were philosophy, religion, and the heavier forms of literature.

So we see John C., a fairly normal person but tending on the whole to withdraw from life. He might have become a fairly good teacher; he probably never would have become so neurotic as to be confined to a mental hospital. But his personality was full of little inhibitions, and he certainly had not become freed to develop his creative powers to anything like their full possibility. Like the great majority of people, he would have pushed along through life carrying such an internal burden of inhibitions and petty conflicts that he would have ended up merely "John C., a little above average."

A year after our consultations I received a letter from him saying,

> I've had a swell time in school this last year; better than during any other year. Do you remember the series of talks we had a year ago relative to my outlook on life? Well, they've made a huge difference in me this year, in more ways than one; and though I still have my Blue Mondays, I think I've taken some long strides in overcoming the deep-set ego-centricity which was my great nemesis a year ago. I've dropped many of my prejudices and fears: I've crawled quite a ways out of my shell. Even Hank, who has been my room-mate this year, has more than once remarked the general change he has noticed in me. And I am finding this matter of "putting away childish things" a heck of a lot of fun.

When I next met him he had been elected president of an important student organization and was in New York attending an intercollegiate conference and meeting influential people with zest and enjoyment. He appeared to have been "freed"; and his personality, like all freed personalities, was developing by geometric progression.

## Chapter II

## A PICTURE OF PERSONALITY

WHAT IS A MAN? Here our constructive discussion must begin, for the effectiveness of counseling with human beings depends upon our understanding of what those human beings really are. A man is more than his body, more than his job, more than his social position. These are but aspects through which he expresses himself. The totality of this expression is the external mirror of that inner structure which we call, somewhat vaguely, "personality." European psychologists would use the term "soul" in this connection as a translation of "psyche"; but for us in America the word "personality" expresses more accurately, no doubt, that basic nature of a human being which makes him a person.

And so we must begin by determining a concept of personality. If the counselor neglects doing this consciously, he will do it nevertheless unconsciously—unwittingly working on the assumption, for example, that his counselee should develop a personality just like his own, or like that of his particular hero, or like the personality ideal of his particular culture. The wise counselor will not leave this basic matter to the vagaries of his unconsciousness, but will consciously and reasonably draw up his picture of personality.

For the sake of clarity let us state our conclusion before we begin; namely, that personality is characterized by *freedom, individuality, social integration, and religious tension.* These are the four principles, as the following discussion will indicate, which are essential to human personality. To make a more complete definition it could be stated: personality is an actualization of the life-process in a free individual who is socially integrated and possesses religious tension.

In forming a picture of personality we must consider the various pictures presented by the modern authorities in the field, the psychotherapists.[1] We begin with the most famous and original of them, Sigmund Freud.[2]

### I. IS PERSONALITY DETERMINISTIC?

THE DETERMINISTIC PICTURE of personality is represented most vividly and persuasively in Freudian psychoanalysis. Unquestionably Freud will go down in history as one of the most influential thinkers of our century. He is a watershed in the history of man's endeavor to understand himself. Indeed, Freud has to an extent robbed man of the luxury of being hypocritical and dishonest—which partly explains why he has been so bitterly attacked.

Freud was born into an age which was calling for psychoanalysis. The nineteenth century had so parceled up human nature, had so compartmentalized life and reduced moral living to a matter of superficial decisions, that Freud's psychoanalysis was greatly needed. Only thus can the wide influence of psychoanalysis be explained. Freud came along to show us that there was much more to personality than our little systems had allowed. He discovered the "depth" in human nature as contained in the profound and powerful realms of the unconsciousness. His centering upon sex as the most influential of human instincts, while too extreme a position to be true in detail, is an inevitable reaction from the hypocritical Victorian moralism which had assumed it could ignore the sex factor in life, cut it out and throw it away, and then go blithely on in "innocence."

In his exploration among men's motives in the unconsciousness, Freud poked up much that was too ugly to be palatable to a generation which had tried to settle all questions in the "immediate center of decision," shelving moral matters by the signing of cards and international problems by the signing of treaties. Freud showed us the ugly side of human nature. If anyone still believes that human nature does not have an ugly side—represented in primitive lusts and savage cruelties—let him merely look at the war-torn state of the modern world. Our narcissism has led us to condemn Freud as a purveyor of slander and smut; but "it is only a great idealist," as the ex-apostle Jung says, "who could have given his life to the uncovering of so much dirt."

Freud is an analytical genius. And he has invented a system for analyzing human personality, which he terms psychoanalysis, which teaches us as counselors much of value about the function of the human mind, though we never, of course, use the system as such.[3] He observed that the adjustments within the individual's mind can be thrown into chaotic disorder by "repressions." These repressions actually represent the individual's being dishonest with himself. The process is somewhat as follows: an instinctual urge pushes up from the "id" (the seething cauldron in the unconsciousness of desires and fears and instinctual tendencies and every sort of psychic content) and seeks expression in the outside world. But the ego, which stands at the threshold of consciousness and mediates between the id and the outside world, is aware of society's prohibitions against the expression of this particular desire, and so it resorts to some ruse to repress the desire. The ruse is a trick by which the ego says to itself, "I don't want to express this desire anyway," or "I'll do this instead." But the repression only means that the urge will come pushing out again in another form—this time in some neurotic symptom such as anxiety or embarrassment or forgetfulness or even some serious form of psychosis.

When a neurotic patient comes to take treatment with a Freudian psychoanalyst, the analyst sets him to verbalizing his mental associations, which means practically talking at random. During this "confession," as it is termed, the analyst lies in wait for signs of a repression, such as the patient's hesitating at some crucial point or his forgetting or showing embarrassment. Such inhibitions or blockages indicate a disunity in the patient's mind, a lack of ready flow from the unconscious source of instinctual tendencies into the consciousness and thence into reality. These symptoms are buoys which indicate the existence of psychological conflicts underneath. Now it becomes the function of the analyst to trace down this conflict, to bring it out of the unconsciousness into plain sight, and, if it is serious, to relieve it by a process of psychological catharsis called abreaction. The end-result is to disentangle the patient's mental snarls, to free him from his "complex," and thus to re-establish some functional unity in his mind. This liberates him to work out some more satisfactory expression of his instinctual urges in reality. Or if expression is impossible, the patient at least is brought to accept consciously and frankly the necessity for renunciation. The central process of psychoanalysis consists of bringing the conflict out of the dark unconsciousness into the light of consciousness where it can be recognized and reasonably handled. "Our usefulness," says Freud, "consists in re-

47

placing the unconscious by the conscious, in translating the unconscious into the conscious." [4]

Among the valuable contributions this system of psychoanalysis makes to our understanding of the human mind is, first, the insight it affords into the tremendous extent and potency of the realm of the unconscious. The exploration of this dark hinterland out of which arise the great forces and motives of life has placed our understanding of man on a much sounder basis. Psychoanalysis shows, also, that we must take much more into our consideration than the conscious ego. This poor "general" has a precarious time of it at best, being buffeted about by the instinctual forces from the id, the outside world, and the super-ego (conscience). Living must therefore be oriented to far deeper levels than merely that of the conscious will. And finally, Freudian psychoanalysis proves that we can never succeed in the moral life by so simple a device as mere repression of every tendency which society or our own super-ego finds unpalatable.

But the danger in the Freudian system of analysis arises when it is carried over into a deterministic interpretation of personality as a whole.[5] The system can become simply a scheme of cause and effect: blocked instinctual urge equals repression equals psychic complex equals neurosis. And the cure consists theoretically of merely reversing the process: observe the neurotic symptom, trace down the complex, remove the repression, and then assist the individual to a more satisfactory expression of his instinctual urges. We do not mean to say that Freudian therapy as it is practiced is as simple as this; the therapy has many more creative aspects, and it succeeds precisely because it does not bind itself to the strict causological theory. But the danger lies in the influence of Freudian theory in setting up a mechanistic, deterministic view of personality in the minds of the partially informed public, so that people conclude that they are the victims of their instinctual drives and that their only salvation lies in expressing their libido whenever the urge arises.

To be sure, the cause-and-effect system is valid for certain aspects of mind. But it is an error to draw generalizations from this limited area which imply that causological, deterministic principles explain the whole of personality. Freud is seduced by the handy, tangible systemization of natural science; and he uses it as a Procrustean bed on which he lays the human personality and forces it to fit.[6] This is the fallacy, all too common in recent decades, which arises out of a failure to recognize the limits of the scientific method. Though the objectivity of science aids us greatly in coming to a useful understanding of certain phases of human mental phenomena, to imagine that the whole of the creative, oftentimes unpredictable, certainly intangible, aspects of human mind can be reduced to cause-and-effect, mechanistic principles is sheer folly. Consequently Freud's "natural science psychology," as Rank calls it, is led astray in its theories of ultimate determinism in personality.

If such a determinism is accepted, human responsibility is destroyed. The thief can say, as Kunkel points out, "Not I but my hunger stole the apple." What of purpose and freedom and creative decision on the part of the individual? These things are basic in personality as we shall observe below.

As a matter of fact, one of the basic presuppositions in all psychotherapy is that the patient must sooner or later accept responsibility for himself. Therefore personal determinism, which excuses him from responsibility, works in the end directly against his regaining mental health. Cause-and-effect determinism holds only for a limited area, namely, the area of the repression-complex neurosis; and when the patient is freed from the complex, he becomes responsible for creatively working out his own future destiny.

Neurotic persons, in my experience, are often precisely the ones who tend to hold a deterministic outlook on life. They seek to blame something else for their difficulties—their parents, or their childhood environment, or their associates; "anything," they seem to be pleading, "so long as I am not to blame." This is understandable, for if they once admitted their own responsibility, they would be forced to take steps to overcome the neurosis. There are, of course, an infinite number of determining factors in any personality difficulty; but underneath all there lies in the individual's own autonomy a point of responsibility and possibility for creative development—and this is the significant factor.

A middle-aged man, manager of a small business in a village, with whom I recently dealt, was in the habit of arguing determinism with great vehemence. He cited experiments with monkeys and every sort of far-fetched pseudo-scientific parallel, and seemed bent by hook or crook to prove that man was no more responsible for his actions than were Pavlov's dogs for the appearance of saliva in their mouths when the appropriate stimulus was given. When a person argues as though his life depends on it, incidentally, you may be sure that more than objective interest in truth lies behind his passion. He is probably trying to save his own neurotic scheme from disturbance. Surely enough, it turned out that this man had failed consistently in a number of jobs since graduating from college. He spoke of his college with embarrassment, and then only to point out that college education does one little good in life. This man, we may conclude, *had* to believe in determinism so long as he failed in his own life. It was his excuse; it relieved him of the oppressive burden of his sense of failure. He was determined to be a determinist *by his mistakes*. But the very vehemence of his arguing gave proof of his subconscious guilt feeling about his failures, and hence he argued determinism precisely because he had a deep conviction that he was not entirely determined.

Yes, determinism does operate in some cases, but these are the neurotic cases. Neurosis means a surrendering of freedom, a giving of one's self over to rigid training formulae; and consequently the personality does become a machine at that point. But mental health means a regaining of one's sense of personal responsibility and hence of one's freedom.

## II. FREEDOM IN PERSONALITY

FREEDOM is a basic principle, in fact a *sine qua non*, of personality. For it is by this characteristic that we separate human beings from animals, the human being having the ability to break the rigid chain of stimulus and response which enslaves animals. The healthy mind is able to hold different impulses in a state of undecided balance and finally to give the decision by which one of the impulses prevails. This possession of creative possibilities, which is synonymous with freedom, is the first presupposition of human personality.

It is not our purpose here to delve into the philosophical proofs of human freedom, but only to point out that from the psychological point of view it is essential to believe in freedom in order to have an adequate picture of personality on which to do effective counseling. This ought not to be called "freedom of the will," for that implies that a particular *part* of man is free, and it results in endless discussions about metaphysical determinism which get us nowhere.[7]   Rather, a man possesses freedom as a quality of his total being.   This is not to say, let it be remembered, that there are not an infinite number of determining influences playing upon the individual from all sides at all moments—many more determining forces than the last century with its emphasis on simple "effort" ever realized.   But regardless of how many determining forces affect John Doe, there is in the end an element by which John Doe molds the materials of heredity and environment into his own unique pattern.   Arguing against freedom only proves it the more firmly; for an argument, in fact any sort of reasonable discussion or even the asking of questions, presupposes this margin of freedom.

Students often come to the counselor and defend a certain irresponsible point of view on the basis of smatterings of natural science to which they have been exposed sufficiently to see the force but not the limitations.   If a personality problem is at stake, the counselor will not argue the question directly—counseling is never argument.   But he will point out possibilities, and thus gradually bring the student to an acceptance of responsibility for his conduct and his future.

The psychotherapist Otto Rank has definitively explained the importance of freedom and responsibility in psychotherapy.[8]   Long one of Freud's closest associates, Rank was finally forced to break with the master because of Freud's refusal to admit the centrality of creative will in the psychoanalytic treatment.[9]   Rank holds that in the long last we must admit that the individual creates his own personality by creative willing, and that neurosis is due precisely to the fact that the patient cannot will constructively.[10]

It is possible to grow in freedom.   The more mentally healthy the person becomes, the more he is able to mold creatively the materials of life, and hence the more he has appropriated his potentiality of freedom. When the counselor, therefore, helps the counselee to overcome his personality difficulty, he has actually helped him to become more free.

To summarize our first principle of personality, freedom, in the form of a guide for counseling: *It is the function of the counselor to lead the counselee to an acceptance of responsibility for the conduct and outcome of his life.* The counselor will show him how deep lie the roots of decision, how all previous experience and the forces of the unconscious must be reckoned with; but in the end he will aid the counselee to appropriate and use his possibilities of freedom.

### III. INDIVIDUALITY IN PERSONALITY

THE SECOND PRINCIPLE which is basic in personality is individuality. The person who comes to the counselor with a personality problem has his difficulty because he cannot be himself—cannot, in other words, individuate. "The neurotic type," Rank pertinently says, "which we all represent to a certain extent, suffers from the fact that he cannot accept himself, cannot endure himself, and will have it otherwise." [11]

For in the end the person has only himself through which to live and face the world. If he cannot be himself he certainly cannot assume any other self no matter how greatly he may wish to do so. His self is different from every other self; it is unique, and healthiness of mind depends upon his accepting this uniqueness.

Consider the infinite variety in persons! A crowd in Times Square appears to move like a stream of marbles, each one wearing the same weary poker-face—but look beneath the protective mask and how wonderfully variegated and unique are the aspects of each individual! The counselor will be continually amazed by the uniqueness and originality of each story told him. Sometimes after a fatiguing series of interviews I find myself subconsciously assuming that I must have met all possible types of persons and that the next one will be only a boring repetition. But scarcely has this next one progressed a few sentences in his story till I realize that here is an exciting novel I have never read. One is overcome in wonder at God's resourcefulness in creating them "male and female" and everyone different. The counselor feels like crying with the psalmist, "When I consider thy heavens, the work of thy fingers. . . . . What is man? . . . . For thou hast made him but little lower than God, and crownest him with glory and honor." It is this uniqueness of each person that we as counselors seek to preserve. The function of the counselor is to help the counselee be what God intended him to be.

The mistakes in life occur when the individual tries to act some other role than his own. The student who inveterately says the wrong thing at social functions is not to be pigeonholed as inherently tactless; he may be possessed of an inner fear which makes him try to act a role that is not his—and of course the result is blunder. Many instances of young people slipping into loose sexual practices are to be understood as a result of their fear of being themselves and their consequent desperate clutching at another role. It is often after the party where she has not been a social success that a girl makes her sexual mistakes. Getting drunk, it is obvious, is a form of escaping one's self. When a young man gets half "tight" before a party, he is arranging things so that he will not have to be himself at the party. The pertinent question is not, why is he so evil as to drink? but rather, why does he feel he has to flee from himself? It follows that we should set up a social program for our young people in which they can be themselves and get satisfaction from it. Such social functions would be the best kind of exercise in personality health.

It is self-evident that psychotherapy works fundamentally on this principle of individuality. Rank explains it as the aim of his method: "To say it in one word, the aim is self-development; this is, the person is to develop himself into that which he is." [12]

The definitive statement on the subject of individuality comes from the renowned Swiss psychologist, C. G. Jung. His work, entitled *Psychological Types*, was so pertinent to modern needs that his terms "introvert" and "extrovert" have become common parlance. The extrovert is that type of individual who lives in such a way as to correspond with objective conditions, or demands that originate outside himself; he tends, like the business man or soldier, to emphasize activity.[13] The introvert, on the other hand, is oriented primarily to subjective data; poets and philosophers and lovers of scientific research tend to fall in this category. There is, of course, no hard and fast line; we all have more or less introvertive and extrovertive tendencies. Jung realizes that his system, which he develops much more intricately than here indicated, is simply a frame of reference which gives very general pointer readings. It is neither right nor fruitful to pigeonhole people. Jung himself, significantly, is the psychotherapist who most emphasizes individuality. It is helpful if we keep a very pliable frame of categories for reference, but let it be remembered that in the end there must be a unique category for every individual.

In America there is a tendency to identify extroversion with personality health and introversion with illness. We Americans tend to be extroverts because of our pio-

neer, activist background and our present preoccupation
with business and industry, linked with an underemphasis,
especially in the past, on cultural pursuits. This is the
mischievous error of assuming that *our* particular type is
the only healthy type. The youth who is essentially the
artist, or the reflective philosopher, or the devotee of scientific research may be made psychologically unhealthy by
being pushed into the position of a commercial salesman.
Of course the caution against becoming *too* introvertive
is sound, and it is even more dangerous to be too introvertive than too extrovertive, for society can be depended
upon to help beat the extrovert off his egocentric tangents.
But the ultimate aim is that the individual find his own
unique role.

The most vicious mistake many counselors make is in
trying to compress their counselees into a particular type—
usually the type to which the counselor himself belongs.
The counselor did not join a fraternity in college, and so
he assumes it is better that the student not join. The professor studied his undergraduate head off, and so he may
advise the sophomore to let up on social activities and
plunge into his books. These are crude examples, but the
point will be clear; namely, that there is always a vicious
tendency for the counselor to view the counselee in terms
of his own attitudes, moral standards, and general personality pattern, and consequently to project these upon the
counselee, thus violating the autonomy of the counselee's
individuality. The technique of unmasking and guarding
against this tendency will be discussed in a later chapter.

There is good ground, then, for the advice so often
bandied about, "be yourself." But it does little good simply to tell the person to be himself, for the trouble is
precisely that he does not know which self he really is.
The counselee often feels within himself a number of con-

flicting "selves," and to tell him merely to be himself is to make confusion worse confounded. He must first *find* himself—and this is where the counselor comes in.

The counselor's function is to help the counselee find what Aristotle speaks of as "entelechy," the unique form in the acorn which destines it to grow into an oak. "Each of us carries his own life-form," says Jung, "an indeterminable form which cannot be superseded by another." [14] This life-form, the real self, reaches into depths in the individual's mind far below ordinary consciousness; consciousness may even present a distorted mirroring of it. The individual finds himself by uniting his conscious self with various levels in his unconsciousness.

At this point it is necessary to describe and define more clearly this important realm of the unconscious. Everyone has experienced the fact that only a small portion of his mental content is conscious at any given moment. Mental content moves through consciousness in a stream—possibly to be compared with the moving of a film in a reel across the light of a movie projector which throws an ever-changing picture on the screen. The old simile has it that the conscious portion of mind compares to the unconscious as the tip of the iceberg rising out of the water compares to the much larger bulk of it floating under the surface. Certainly our minds reach infinitely deeper than any momentary area of consciousness—how deep we cannot determine, for unconscious means "unknown." We can only postulate the unconscious and observe how it manifests itself functionally. Persons who have become habituated to thinking only in the limited terms of calculable science sometimes hesitate to postulate the unconscious; but to do that is to cut off the great bulk of our mental life. For what of all the memories, past experiences, knowledge, *ad infinitum* which are not in our conscious minds at this particular instant but which we could summon there at a moment's notice? No experience is ever lost, theoretically. Nothing is really forgotten, and childhood experiences leave their force upon the person even though he may shrug his shoulders and think the matter lost and gone forever. Memory and forgetfulness and other problems of the unconscious are intricate matters, and there is still much knowledge to be gained about them.

Our functional interpretation pictures the unconscious as a great storehouse including every sort of psychic content: fears, hopes, desires, and all kinds of instinctual tendencies. But it is a dynamo even more than a storehouse, for out of it come the drives and tendencies which consciousness merely directs. "The great decisions of life," Jung rightly says, "have as a rule far more to do with the instincts and other mysterious unconscious factors than with the conscious will and well-meaning reasonableness." [15]

The unconscious may be viewed as a series of levels. This concept corresponds with actual experience, for an experience of childhood seems to be much "deeper" than one of yesterday. Freud speaks of the "preconscious" as that portion of the unconscious just below consciousness. We may term this preconscious material that can rise immediately to consciousness, plus childhood experiences and repressed material, the "personal unconscious."

As we plumb deeper into the unconscious we find more and more material which the individual possesses in common with other individuals. Jung gives the useful term "collective unconscious" to these deeper levels. The Frenchman or the citizen of the United States, for example, holds much material in his unconscious which he did not experience himself, but which he absorbs from his national group. This will have a certain connection with the history of the national group, but it is transmitted in much deeper ways than through history classrooms and text-books. The pioneer experiences of early Americans carry through with some force into the unconscious of a modern American, though the latter is several generations removed from the actual pioneer life. In primitive societies where the collective consciousness is greater, it is quite difficult to tell where the experiences of the forefathers leave off and those of the present begin. An even deeper stratum of the unconscious is that which we possess in common with all other members of our race, or deeper still, that held collectively by members of the western world.

And, finally, there are certain patterns in the uncon-scious which the individual possesses in common with all mankind. Jung calls these "archetypes" or "primordial images"—defined as the patterns or ways of thought which a man possesses simply because he is a man. These arche-types have a relationship to the basic structure of man's mind. This explains why mythology, though springing up among peoples of diverse races and periods in history, ex-hibits certain common patterns.

Is the collective unconscious inherited or acquired from one's culture? Jung's answer is direct: "We mean by collective unconscious, a certain psychic deposition shaped by the forces of heredity." [16] As a matter of fact, the source of the collective unconscious is not the per-tinent problem; we observe how it works functionally, and it certainly is true from this viewpoint that these basic ideas, as they appear even in the mythological creations of chil-dren, come from something deeper and more organic than what the individual could have learned from his educators. Specific ideas, of course, are acquired from one's environ-ment, and we are not arguing here that all human ideas are "innate." But there must be something structural in mind comparable to the structural form of body which would develop along certain general lines even though the individual were isolated on Crusoe's island. Plato was wrestling with this same difficult problem of describing the function of the collective unconscious when he explained, mythologically, that man is born with certain ideas which carry over from his previous existence in heaven. And so Plato held knowledge to be a reminiscence or a process of tapping what is already deep in one's unconscious.[17]

Great poetry and art and philosophy and religion spring out of this collective unconscious of humanity. The great artist, like Aeschylus or Dante or Shakespeare, taps these deep levels of human sorrow and joy and fear and hope, and serves as an artesian well through which eternal patterns spring into expression.[18] A classic in literature or art is the expression of psychic images which the individual possesses in common with all other men. A classic is thus universal; it is archetypal. In a later section we shall discuss the implications of the locating of religion in the collective unconscious. Here let us only note that "conscience" is given a new validity. Conscience is something more than a residue of one's parents' teachings, more than an expression of social solidarity; it reaches far back into the mysterious sources of our being.

To get back to the individual who comes to the counselor with a personality difficulty. He needs to find his true self, and this is accomplished through his arriving at some degree of unity of his consciousness with the unconscious levels of his childhood experience, the deeper levels of the collective unconscious, and ultimately with that source of his mind which is in the very structure of the universe. It now becomes clear why the neurotic individual can never be healthy as long as he blames his childhood training for his trouble; for he *is* to some extent that childhood training, and in fighting it he is fighting himself. And likewise the individual who is continually at war with society can never attain personality health, for he is struggling against certain forces in the collective unconscious of his own mind.

Finally, he who struggles against the universe, who denies meaning in the universe and tries to break off his connection with it, as do the agnostics and atheists, is actually struggling against the deepest point in himself where he is connected with the universe. This is another way of saying that the individual has the roots of his collective unconscious in that creative structure of the universe which we call God. The genuine atheist would logically exhibit neurotic tendencies (as we find to be actually the case in real instances), for in dueling against God he is actually stabbing the rapier into the deepest portions of his own soul. Discussion of this important matter must be reserved for the final chapter. Suffice it to say here that when the individual truly finds himself, he finds his society, and in one respect he finds God.

From the second principle of personality, individuality, we derive this guide for counseling: *It is the function of the counselor to assist the counselee to find his real self, and then to help him to have courage to be this self.*

## IV. SOCIAL INTEGRATION

PERSONALITY cannot be understood apart from its social setting. For this social setting—the community of other persons—gives personality a world without which it would have no meaning. The social setting furnishes the pegs to which personality attaches the lines of tension of its web, to carry through the simile of the last chapter. We know this to be true in our own experience, for each of us uses other persons as pivot points; we pivot around our enemies as well as around our friends.

Thus the third aspect of healthy personality is *social integration*. So important has this aspect been considered that people have fallen into the habit of assuming that personality difficulty means social difficulty, and that if an individual is a social success he must have solved his personality problems. This of course presupposes a too superficial view of personality—as when the word is profaned in cosmetic and cheap "how-to-be-a-social-success" advertisements. But profoundly viewed, a meaningful social adjustment is basic in personality; for the person must move in a world which consists of other people.

A chief characteristic of the neurotic is his inability to get along with other people. He is highly suspicious of others. He feels society to be his enemy, and he moves through life as though in an armored car. A man recently explained to me that he had spent his vacation trying to get away from his relatives, and then remarked incidentally, "I never trust anyone." Even though this is a common remark, it is a bona fide sign of a neurotic attitude toward society. Such an individual is bound to be lonely, for he forces himself into as isolated and comfortless a position as a machine-gunner fighting all for himself on a mountain-top.

In this matter of social integration we are most indebted to Alfred Adler,[19] that other Viennese who, with Frued, has made Vienna the mother city of psychotherapy. Dr. Adler noticed in his early psychological work in the first years of this century that the neurotic is especially characterized by his inability to make connections with other people and the social world. Adler observed, too, that no one can separate himself from his social group and remain healthy; for the very structure of his personality is dependent upon the community. The child would not have been born except for a social act on the part of its parents, and it could not have survived a day without the care of the family. At any given instant, every individual is dependent upon countless other persons of his age and every previous age. To get a vivid glimpse of this social interdependence, simply call to mind the long train of persons upon whom you are dependent for the bread on your dinner table, or for your ability to say the multiplication table. We live in a social constellation in which every individual is dependent upon every other individual just as the stars in the solar constellations hang upon the lines of gravitational force emanating from every other heavenly body. In fact, this web of interdependence theoretically includes every individual who lives or ever lived. Even though a person may deny this interdependence and fight against it like Nietzsche, he is still dependent on it in the very act of attacking it. The sense of interdependence is continually cropping up out of the collective unconscious of the misanthropic individual when he refuses to admit it consciously. Adler calls this interdependence the "love and logic which bind us all together."

As opposed to Freud's concept of sex libido, Adler sees the dynamic force in the individual as a striving for power. There is an urge within the individual (in the center of the self which we term the "ego") to gain superiority over his fellows, to attain a position of security which cannot be threatened.[20] This is similar to, but not identical with, the "will to power" concepts of such philosophers as Nietzsche and Schopenhauer; but Adler's "will" is more a "will to prestige." It is that basic impulse in the individual which makes him tend to break out the web of social interdependence and set himself, by competitive ambition and vanity, above his fellowmen.[21]

This brings us to the most famous contribution of Adlerian psychology to modern thought, the concept of inferiority. The inferiority feeling (it should not be called "complex" until it has become definitely neurotic) is universal. Every individual has it as part of his function as a human being. John Doe feels inferior to the people around him at a social function and is embarrassed (he forgets that they, too, feel inferior to him). The Browns feel inferior to the Joneses across the street, and hence the great striving to "keep up with the Joneses." Salesman Black has a feeling of inferiority about his job and so becomes jealous of others' successes; and the business world, shot through with every businessman's effort to climb over the others, becomes a melee of merciless competition. We have observed in the previous chapter how the strong inferiority feeling in George B. threw his personality tensions out of adjustment and led to his striving to dominate all others. It is surprising what Olympian forms the inferiority feeling assumes. The dog who is afraid, Aesop would say, is the one who barks most ferociously.

This universal inferiority feeling has its roots in the real inferiority of the infant, who sees the adults around him walking and lifting things and exerting power which he lacks. It is also traceable in part to the real inferiority of primitive man as he strove against animals. Tooth for tooth and claw for claw, man was an easy prey for animals; and hence it was necessary that he compensate for his physical weakness by mental agility. The development of civilization is to be understood to some extent as compensatory; i.e., a result of man's striving to overcome his inferiority.

Since we all have the inferiority feeling, it is not to be considered abnormal in itself. Indeed, coupled with the will to prestige, it furnishes us with our main source of motive power. The problem is to utilize this power, not in anti-social striving which destroys the social constellation, but in constructive effort which contributes to the well-being of our fellows.

But an exaggerated inferiority feeling leads to neurotic behavior because it gives the ego an abnormally strong striving for power. The more "under" or minus the individual feels himself to be, the more desperately will he struggle to put himself "on top." The inferiority feeling and the will to prestige are merely two aspects of the same drive within the individual. Thus we can infer that behind a tremendous ambition there lurks a deep (though possibly unconscious) inferiority feeling. Historical instances prove this time and again. What is called a superiority complex" is for the same reason merely the reverse side of an underlying inferiority feeling—because the ego feels itself inferior, it assumes a special front of superiority and makes sure that everyone notices it.

In this scheme of striving for prestige, the lowering of other persons is equivalent to the raising of the individual himself; for as they go down he automatically gains more superiority. This explains why people derive pleasure from gossiping. Everyone has felt this tendency within himself to lower others for the sake of the raising of his own prestige. The normal individual keeps the tendency under control, and aims to direct his efforts socially; but the neurotic directs his striving antisocially and attempts to climb up a ladder made of other persons. Thus he is warring against the very structure to which he owes his existence. He cuts away his own roots—and such could not help ending in mental ill-health. Adler therefore defines neurosis as anti-social striving for power.

The chief human sins, which are, according to Adler, continually destroying human culture and happiness, are *vanity* and *ambition*, the two expressions of the dominating ego. The latter is difficult to understand in America, for we have made ambition a virtue. What Adler actually means, however, is "antisocial ambition"; and we must agree with him that exaggerated ambition, as it is manifested in the historic conquerors or modern captains of industry, is rooted in the ego's striving for power rather than in the desire to serve humanity.

The normal striving for power should be differentiated from the neurotic. Normal ambition proceeds from strength, is a natural function of the living being, and is not necessarily anti-social; neurotic ambition proceeds from weakness and insecurity, and derives its satisfaction from the debasing and dominating of others.

This brings home the need for courage in healthy living. For when the individual is given courage, he is relieved from the compulsion of his inferiority feeling and therefore does not need to strive against others. Fear creates great havoc in human relations. Give the misanthropic individual basic courage, and he finds himself suddenly relieved of much of his insecurity and able to co-operate unselfishly with the group.

In addition to courage, the highest virtues, according to the Adlerian system, are *social interest* and *co-operation*. These mark the healthy individual who realizes and cheerfully accepts his social responsibility. By expressing himself in socially constructive ways he is able to achieve and realize himself, whereas the misanthropic individual "seeking to save his life" in egocentric striving actually loses it. The healthy individual becomes socially "integrated," which literally means attaining "wholeness." He "renews" his primordial position as an organic part of community. Thus he is relieved from neurotic anxieties and little fears and inhibitions. "Only that individual can go through life without anxiety," says Adler, "who is conscious of belonging to the fellowship of man." [22]  Does the second aspect of personality, individuality, militate against social integration?  Not ideally.  As Shakespeare puts it:

> "To thine own self be true,
>   And it must follow, as the night the day,
>   Thou canst not then be false to any man."

Superficially, it is true, there may be a tension between individuality and social integration; to get along with one's neighbors one often has to inhibit certain superficial expressions of individuality.  But more profoundly speaking there is not the incompatibility between individuality and social living that people often assume; in the collective unconscious we are united with our fellows even within ourselves. [23]  It is true that there is an egocentric element in man which makes it very difficult for him to be genuinely social, as will be discussed later; but this egocentric element also destroys his unity within himself.  Practically speaking, counselors will find that the more socially integrated the counselee becomes, the more, on the whole, he will realize his unique individuality.

From the third principle of personality, social integration, we derive this guide for counseling:  *It is the counselor's function to assist the counselee to a cheerful acceptance of his social responsibility, to give him courage which will release him from the compulsion of his inferiority feeling, and to help him to direct his striving toward socially constructive ends.*

## V. RELIGIOUS TENSION

EARLIER in this chapter we have spoken of the psychoanalytic view that mental illness consists of a disunity in the mind of the patient and the psychological conflicts which follow from this. And we have mentioned that the aim of psychoanalysis was to re-unify mental life by bringing the conflict out of the unconscious into consciousness.

This emphasis of psychoanalysis upon mental unity has been taken by many people to mean that the more unity one can achieve in one's personality, the healthier one is, that the ideal is a final unity, and that psychological conflicts are therefore unhealthy in themselves. The Jungian emphasis upon the unifying of the individual's consciousness with various substrata in his unconscious, and the Adlerian goal of integration of the individual with society, likewise lend themselves to the interpretation that a unity within the mind of the individual is the ultimate *desideratum*.

It is perfectly true that the neurotic person suffers from a breakdown in unity of his mental functions, and it is likewise self-evident that guiding him back to a more effective adjustment with its accompanying condition of new unity is a step in the cure. But it is not true that a simple and ultimate unity within personality is the ideal. The amateur devotees of psychotherapy and a portion of the public at large, down to which a smattering of the ideas of psychoanalysis has percolated, misinterpret psychotherapy and oversimplify personality when they assume that the goal is a state of complete relaxation, in which one can readily express all his instinctual desires in reality and live the life of the lotus eaters or the inhabitants of the Mohammedan heaven. Some people tend to think that the aim of psychotherapy is to put everyone into a Garden of Eden where all urges are satisfied and one wanders about in a bliss which is undisturbed by moral and psychological conflict. All this is of course quite foreign to the human situation, and no reputable psychotherapist would admit such an ideal.

A final unity in the human personality is neither possible nor desirable. Existence in the Garden of Eden or in the heavens of the blissful and placid type would mean death to personality as we know it. For personality is dynamic, not static; creative, not vegetative. What we desire is a new and constructive adjustment of tensions rather than any final unity. We do not wish to wipe away conflict altogether—that would be stagnation—but rather *to transform destructive conflicts into constructive ones.*

It must be admitted that the psychotherapists have given room for this popular misinterpretation. Freud has given room for it in his natural science presuppositions and his tendency to reduce personality to cause-and-effect determinism. Adler has similarly erred in his rationalistic faith in the idea that knowledge will lead to virtue. There are certain rationalistic, romantic, naturalistic presuppositions underlying the historical development of psychotherapy which lend themselves to this oversimplification. The temptation is to view personality as something which grows as simply and naturally as plants, as is illustrated in the remark of a therapist of the Adlerian school who defined the function of psychotherapy: "To remove the obstructions from the path of the personality as you remove the stones obstructing the growth of a flower, thus letting the flower grow up naturally toward the sun." Such a confidence in the natural growing of the human being toward his perfect state reminds us of Rousseau, and it is certainly to be viewed as a romantic faith lacking sufficient realism.

This tendency toward oversimplification is evidenced in the handling of the problem of *guilt feeling.* Some psychotherapists aim to wipe away guilt feeling entirely, treating it as a symptom of mental ill-health, and reproaching religion for increasing the morbid guilt feeling of many people. To be sure, they are right in the respect that exaggerated guilt feeling is often connected with neurosis, and also that unenlightened religion has altogether too often abetted morbid guilt feeling in its adherents. An example of the latter is the case of a minister who was burdened for twenty-seven years by an obsession of sin which turned out in the end to be purely subjective and without relation to reality. It is quite understandable that Freud, specializing in sexual phenomena, should treat guilt feeling as unhealthy, because the nineteenth century had attached a tremendous amount of morbid guilt to sexual phenomena.[24] Psychotherapists and counselors will unite in the endeavor to free people from morbid guilt feeling.

But guilt feeling can never be wiped away entirely, nor would it be desirable to do so. There is a normal element of it that is compatible with, yes, even necessary for, personality health.

Let us get more clearly in mind what guilt feeling is. It is not to be defined in such negative terms as is the tendency in our utopian-minded culture. Guilt feeling is actually a positive, constructive emotion. It is a perception of the difference between what a thing is and what it ought to be. Everyone experiences a guilt feeling an infinite number of times a day. When one passes a cripple begging on the street or a drunken man in the gutter, when by neglect or conscious deed one does harm to another person, when one is aware of war going on even in another country—in short, the individual experiences guilt feeling whenever he has a feeling of "ought," a sense of the discrepancy between what he is and what he ought to be, or what he does and what he ought to do, or what the situation is and what it ought to be. This should not be confused with "conscience"—guilt feeling is the much broader aspect of human experience of which conscience is one expression. In the example of the beggar, the guilt feeling does not depend on whether or not one gives him money: it may be sociologically better not to give; but the feeling of guilt inheres in the realization that here is a situation—a human being degraded into begging—which is far from any norm or ideal of human living.

If there were any act in life in which the individual could attain unity in self and thus transcend the guilt feeling, it would be the act of pure creativity such as occurs in that most intense moment in painting when the artist is carried up into a kind of ecstasy. But artists very often have the most poignant and vivid feeling of guilt about their work. While he is intensely engrossed in painting, the creative process seems to grasp the artist and carry him along like a chip on a wave with such speed that he is for the moment conscious of nothing outside the creative act itself. But when the picture is finished he has two emotions: one is the satisfaction and the sense of psychological catharsis which all creative effort brings; the other is the guilt feeling, bathed and made even more distinct in outline by the catharsis. This guilt feeling is first a realization that the picture is not as perfect as it should be; i.e., that it falls short of the ideal vision the painter had in mind. And in the second and more significant respect, it is a realization that something great has taken place which the artist did not merit. Great artists have this curious realization that they are dealing with something dangerous.[25] They have come for a moment to the porch of beauty itself, and the reaction is like that in primitive religions when touching the altar of God made one guilty.

One has only to look through classical literature, mythologies of various peoples, and primitive religions to discover how universal is this guilt feeling among men. The ancient Greeks were certainly not a morbid people—indeed, it is often said that they did not know the meaning of our word "sin"—yet this realization of guilt runs centrally through their dramas and gives them their profound meaning. The implication is that this guilt is inherent in man's situation; man is stationed below the gods, said the Greek dramatists, but he is always tending to raise himself to the divine position.

What is the source of guilt feeling? In the first place, we can immediately see why it is inescapable in personality, for it is inseparably connected with freedom, autonomy, and moral responsibility. "Free will," Rank aptly says, "belongs to the idea of guilt or sin as inevitably as day to night." [26] Since the individual possesses creative freedom, he must all the time be glimpsing new possibilities; and every new possibility brings with it not only a challenge but an element of guilt feeling. In fact, challenge—the movement toward achieving the new possibility—and guilt feeling are two aspects of the same thing. Guilt feeling inheres in every state of tension in personality. Guilt feeling is the perception of a "gap"; it is, to use a crude simile, as though one were standing over a deep cleft in a mountain with one foot on one side and one on the other.

Poets and philosophers and theologians have wrestled through the ages with the problem of explaining this curious guilt feeling in the depths of man's being. Some have concluded that its source lies in the gap between perfection and man's imperfect state: man wants to paint a perfect picture or write a perfect poem, for example; but because he is fated to an existence in the human realm where everything is imperfect, he always falls short of his goal. Other thinkers, particularly the poets, have said that this guilt feeling has its source in the conflict between the animal and the spiritual natures of man. Greek Platonic thought makes it the conflict between body and mind. The psychotherapist Fritz Kunkel locates the guilt feeling in the subject-object tension within the individual. Rank holds that it arises from man's moral self-consciousness, and he cites the Biblical story of the fall to prove this. When Adam ate of the "tree of the knowledge of good and evil"—which signified the birth of his capacity to perceive the difference between right and wrong—he began to feel shame and guilt.

However we attempt to explain this guilt feeling, we must admit that it proves that there is some contradiction in man's nature. It means that man is both of the earth and of the spirit, to use popular but inaccurate terms. It means that if man tries to live only in earthy, natural terms, like the animals, he becomes neurotic; and if he tries to escape entirely into the spiritual world and deny that he has a body—as spiritualism and certain extreme forms of Christian Science do—he also becomes neurotic. This situation is what people in past ages have had in mind when they spoke of man's being "caught between two worlds." It is in reality not a matter of *two* worlds, but of two aspects of the same world; and this is precisely what makes the problem so complicated. For man must hold within himself the tension between these two opposite aspects of the world—the unconditioned and the conditioned. Man is not a horizontal creature entirely, nor a vertical creature; he lives both horizontally and vertically.[27] And the intersecting of these two planes is what causes the basic tension in man. No wonder his life cannot be a simple unity!

Out of this ultimate tension comes man's religion. At the point of intersection between the vertical and horizontal arises man's sense of the absolute moral commands which Kant and many other thinkers have emphasized. At this point man also gets his conception of perfection: behind or implied in the imperfect beauty of a particular tree or painting, for example, man glimpses the form of perfect beauty.

The contradiction in man, thus, is proof of the presence of God in human nature. The Christian way of expressing the tension is in terms of man's sonship to God. Man as we know him existentially is conditioned, finite, imperfect; but he is essentially connected with God, and this relationship brings in the elements of the unconditioned, the infinite and perfect. In the light of such a tension, it is perfectly understandable that man should experience some guilt feeling at every moment; for it is the manifestation of God's continual impingement upon man's temporal life.

So guilt feeling, far from being something morbid for which we are to be ashamed, is actually a proof of our great possibilities and destiny. Man should rejoice in it; for it means that a "spark disturbs our clod." More highly developed personalities feel this sense of guilt more keenly than the average, and utilize it in their further development.

Therefore any picture of personality which leaves out the aspect of religious tension is incomplete. Purely naturalistic psychotherapies will always be inadequate. We can conclude that the healthy individual must have a creative adjustment to God, and that a sound religion is indispensable to personality health.

From the fourth principle of personality, religious tension, this guide for counseling is derived: *It is the counselor's function, while aiding the counselee to free himself from morbid guilt feeling, to assist him courageously to accept and affirm the religious tension inherent in his nature.*

*Chapter III*

EMPATHY–KEY TO THE COUNSELING PROCESS

HAVING DISCUSSED the nature of personality, we are now confronted by the subsequent question of how personality functions. More precisely, how does one personality meet and react upon another? The answer lies in the concept of *empathy*, the general term for the contact, influence, and interaction of personalities.

"Empathy" comes to us as a translation of the word of the German psychologists, "einfulung" which means literally "feeling into." It is derived from the Greek "pathos," meaning a deep and strong feeling akin to suffering, prefixed with the preposition "in." The parallel with the word "sympathy" is obvious. But whereas sympathy denotes "feeling with" and may lead into sentimentality, empathy means a much deeper state of identification of personalities in which one person so feels himself into the other as temporarily to lose his own identity. It is in this profound and somewhat mysterious process of empathy that understanding, influence, and the other significant relations between persons take place. Thus in discussing empathy we are considering not only the key process in counseling, but the key likewise to practically all the work of preachers, teachers, and others whose vocation depends upon the influencing of people.

To begin with an example, let me describe the case of a certain student who came into my office for a counseling interview. He approached rather timidly, shaking my hand in a clammy manner and smiling apologetically. Though large in stature he gave one the impression of a big child, and as he spoke he blushed continually and gazed down at the floor. Soon he was relating in a low, hesitating voice certain occurrences in his childhood and other aspects of his home background that lay behind his present perplexities.

While he talked I sat perfectly relaxed and let my eyes rest on his face. I permitted myself to become absorbed in his story; and soon I was so completely engrossed that I was unconscious of our physical surroundings in the room and aware only of this boy's frightened eyes, his tremulous voice, and the fascinating human drama which he was describing.

He told how his father had used to beat him during his boyhood on the farm, and how he had grown up without parental love or understanding. During this moment I felt the pain of his father's beatings, curious at it may seem, as though I myself were receiving the blows. Then he told of running away to high school, where he had supported himself alone under great handicaps. Through high school he had been burdened by an overpowering sense of inferiority. And as he described this inferiority feeling, a depression occurred in myself as though the inferiority had been my own.

Then the young man spoke of his early wish to come to college, which had been met by his parents' sarcastic prediction that he would not be able to last it a semester. With bulldog determination he had nevertheless arrived on the campus, practically penniless. Since then—he was now a sophomore—he had been working his way while struggling at the same time to keep up in studies for which he was poorly prepared. Speaking then of his college experience, he described the shyness and inferiority feeling which continued to oppress him and the loneliness that he suffered even in the midst of the hurly-burly of campus life.

The point to be observed in this illustration is that the psychic states of the counselee and the counselor were to some extent identified. As counselor I had become so absorbed in his story that his emotions had become my emotions. His feeling of desperation as he struggled through high school, his realization of the loneliness of existence and the harshness of destiny, became my own experiences, felt on my pulse as they had originally been on his. And when he concluded by stating his determination to stick it out at college if it killed him, I felt a certain exhilaration as though this resolution had been made by my own will. This partial identification was so real that if I had spoken aloud my voice would no doubt have partaken of the hesitant, quavering quality of his. The conclusion is forced upon us that the ego or psychic state of the counselor had temporarily become merged with that of the counselee; he and I were one psychic unity.

This is empathy. It is the feeling, or the thinking, of one personality into another until some state of identification is achieved. In this identification real understanding between people can take place; without it, in fact, no understanding is possible. It is clear that the experience of empathy comes into every counselor's day dozens of times, whether it is recognized as such or not. Empathy is not a magical process even though it is mysterious. It appears difficult to understand precisely because it is so common and basic. As Adler points out, this identifying of one's self with the other person takes place to some extent in every conversation. It is the fundamental process in love.

Most persons have never taken the trouble to analyze their capacity to empathize, and consequently they possess the ability only in rudimentary and undeveloped form. But ministers and teachers and others who deal intimately with persons had best endeavor to understand it, for their success depends upon their ability to accomplish this walking with another person into the deepest chambers of his soul.

Empathy is experienced, in the first place, with inanimate objects. The bowler sways in the direction he wishes the ball to roll as though he could influence it with his own body. Whole grandstands of people will heave with a football team, each person bracing himself and grunting as though he himself were making the tackle!

In artistic experience empathy is also basic, for the individual must in some way identify himself with the object if he is to experience it aesthetically. Thus people speak of music "carrying them away," or of the violin playing upon the strings of their emotions, or of the changing colors of the sunset creating a corresponding change in their emotions. Jung makes empathy the center of his theory of aesthetics. The person looking at the artistic object, he says, "becomes the object; he identifies himself with it, and in this way gets rid of himself." [1] This is the secret of the cathartic power of art—the aesthetic experience does actually take the artist or the spectator out of himself. Aristotle has classically described how seeing a great dramatic tragedy purges the soul of the observer, precisely for the reason that the tragedy is enacted on the stage of the observer's own soul as he watches it on the real stage. Drama is the form of art in which empathy is most easily understood; for there occurs the very obvious identification of the actors with the fictitious characters they are representing, as well as the more subtle identification of the observers with the actors.

This cathartic quality, resulting from empathy, is present in good conversation. We even might, in fact, judge the merit of a particular conversation by asking how much it has taken us out of ourselves. Counseling has the cathartic function superlatively. The counselor has to go out of himself almost completely; that is why a period of genuine and intense counseling will leave him curiously freed from his own problems. At the same time he will feel strangely fatigued, just as the artist is fatigued after two hours' painting.

Adler recognizes empathy as one of the creative functions in personality and goes on to say:

Empathy occurs in the moment one human being speaks with another. It is impossible to understand another individual if it is impossible at the same time to identify one's self with him. . . . . If we seek for the origin of this ability to act and feel as if we were someone else, we can find it in the existence of an inborn social feeling. This is, as a matter of fact, a cosmic feeling and a reflection of the connectedness of the whole cosmos which lives in us; it is an inescapable characteristic of being a human being." [2]

Jung describes the *merging* process here involved, both the counselor and the counselee being changed: "The meeting of two personalities is like the contact of two chemical substances; if there is any reaction, both are transformed. We should expect the doctor to have an influence on the patient in every effective psychic treatment; but this influence can only take place when he, too, is affected by the patient." [3]

The original source of the capacity for empathy is found, so far as we can determine, in the ability of primitive peoples to identify themselves with each other and with their community and totem. This is termed "*partici-*

*pation mystique."* Levy-Bruhl, the great French anthropologist who has pursued this subject with particular depth, says that the primitive people identify themselves with each other in such a complete way as to produce a "community of essence" and a *"continuum* of spiritual powers." "A certain community of being is thus immediately felt, not only between members of the same totemic family, but between all entities of any kind whatsoever which form part of the same class and are linked together in mystic fellowship." [4]  The child feels the effect of what its parents eat, and the hunter away in the forest is influenced by what his wife eats or does back in the village. This may seem a far cry from our modern individuality in civilization, but as a matter of fact it is not so. Our assumption that persons can isolate themselves and live their own lives is superficial and illusory; it is a result of the exaggerated attempt to be rational and apply logical separations to life. That man even in civilization is a creature of very collective modes of thought and behavior is proven in modern nationalistic trends. If we had earlier recognized this, we should not now be confronted with such demonic exaggerations of collective psychology as appear in the totalitarian states.

Participation in other persons or objects gives us an understanding of them which is far more intimate and meaningful than mere scientific analysis or empirical observation. For "under-standing," be it of things as different as a rubber ball and a period of history, actually means this identification of subjective and objective resulting in a new condition which transcends them both. Levy-Bruhl adds that this is particularly true in the matter of our knowledge of God. We can never arrive at an understanding of God through purely rational, logical methods; the individual must himself participate in God. The customary term for this method is "faith." Levy-Bruhl describes it more fully as "direct and intimate contact with the essence of being, by intuition, interpenetration, the mutual communion of subject and object, full participation and immanence, in short, that which Plotinus has described as ecstasy." [5]

To know the meaning of beauty or love or any of the so-called values of life, we must let ourselves participate in them. Thus "experiencing" them, we shall know them "on our pulse," as Keats puts it. It is sheer folly to think that another person can be known by analysis or formulae; here understanding as participation comes into its own. In other words, it is impossible to know another person without being, broadly speaking, in love with him. But this state means that both persons will be changed by the identification which the love brings about. Thus it is literally true that love works a change in the personalities of both the lover and the loved. It may tend to make them become more alike, or it may draw the loved one up toward the ideal in the lover's mind. Love therefore carries tremendous psychological power. It is the greatest force available in the influencing and transforming of personality.[6]

The counselor works basically through the process of empathy. Both he and the counselee are taken out of themselves and become merged in a common psychic entity. The emotions and will of each become part of this new psychic entity. Consequently the problem of the counselee is dumped on the "new person," and the counselor then bears his half of it. And the psychological stability of the counselor, his clarity, his courage and strength of will, will carry through to the counselee, thus lending him great assistance in his personality struggle.

Let it be clearly understood that empathy does not

mean identifying one's experiences with the counselee, such as occurs when the counselor remarks, "Yes, that happened to me too when I was such-and-such an age." There is no place in true counseling for the reminiscences of the counselor. All of this comes out of egocentricity, and empathy is precisely the opposite of egocentricity. The previous experiences of the counselor do not come into the counseling situation *as such*. Understanding the counselee according to his own unique pattern is the goal; and if the counselor says or thinks, "I had that problem myself and I met it in such and such a way," he will be projecting himself into the situation in a way which may be very vicious. The counselor's previous experience will aid him immeasurably in understanding the counselee—in this regard previous experience is indispensable; but such experience will contribute indirectly. At the moment of the counseling situation it would be theoretically well if the counselor forgot he ever had any experiences of his own; his function is to give himself up, be almost a *tabula rasa*, surrender himself to the empathetic situation.

### MENTAL TRANSFERENCE

THE QUESTION arises concerning the connection between empathy and mental telepathy, or other special aspects of psychical transference. Mental telepathy denotes a transfer of ideas between persons by means beyond our known senses. It would appear, then, to have clear affinities with the empathetic process.

Empathy is the general term for all participation of one personality in the psychic state of another, and the hypothesis of telepathy refers to one aspect of this participation. The proof of the existence of empathy does not depend on the ultimate substantiation of mental telepathy; for the former occurs, as we have indicated above, in such everyday phenomena as conversation and simple human understanding. But if telepathy is scientifically proven, as it may in some future time be, we shall have a very vivid and cogent illustration of one aspect of the participation of personalities in each other.

Dr. J. B. Rhine's highly significant experiments in clairvoyance and telepathy have recently been published, making available to us the results of probably the most far-reaching experiments in the field of extra-sensory perception in all history.[7] Through careful experimental research for seven years Dr. Rhine has amassed results from hundreds of thousands of tests held under conditions the scientific objectivity of which is, it appears, unimpeachable. The results have been termed "amazing." They clearly prove that so far as these tests were concerned, something was operative over and above the perception of the five senses. This gives evidence, states Dr. Rhine, for the existence of extra-sensory perception which "seems to be a normal part of the integral system of mind." [8] This perception seems to be of a non-physical character, not a "sixth sense" or any physical sense at all.

We are not able on the basis of this evidence to conclude anything final in regard to the existence of telepathy, even though Dr. Rhine's comprehensive work has so far withstood the attacks of mathematicians and psychologists. This matter is in the field of experimental science; and here the intelligent approach is to suspend judgment, awaiting further experimentation and the acceptance of the theory on the part of authorities. There is no denying, however, that Dr. Rhine's experiments have made impossible any easy denial of the possibilities of telepathy and have weighted the balance of judgment in favor of thought transference.

The most significant observation to be made in these

experiments, from our point of view, is that the conditions under which telepathy apparently worked best are precisely those conditions which make for effective empathy. The person taking the test had to have confidence and a hopeful and zestful attitude toward the experiments; "the whole procedure requires confidence and the best of personal relations." [9]    These qualities are likewise the ones upon which empathy depends.   Empathy requires good rapport between the persons concerned, and works ideally between persons in love.   Surely enough, Dr. Rhine's tests indicate a parallel in telepathy, for they worked best between the young man and woman who were shortly thereafter married.   Another point of similarity is that both telepathy and empathy are functions too creative to be controlled to any great extent by conscious willing.   The person taking the tests, for example, could not improve his score simply by putting forth more effort.   In empathy, as a matter of fact, conscious striving may block the process rather than aid it; the most one can do is to make the conditions right and then allow the mind to respond, as when listening to music.   Telepathy, according to Dr. Rhine, appears to be the highest function of mind in the respect that it is most sensitive to stimulants and gives way most quickly to fatigue.   Empathy is certainly also a delicate function of personality and requires by definition a high degree of sensitivity.

Whether one puts great credence in Dr. Rhine's results or not—and we have suggested that from the scientific point of view it is best not yet to draw final conclusions—it is certainly true that much more psychical transference occurs between persons than is ordinarily admitted.   All through history people have had the suspicion that transference of thought by means beyond the word and gesture was occurring even though they could not prove it.

Freud remarks that this is particularly true between children and parents, in which regard a number of instances of telepathy have been, he believes, adequately substantiated.[10] The source of the telepathic processes, Freud suggests, may be a "communal" mind among persons similar to that prevailing among insects, this possibly being the archaic, original method of communication between human beings.

It would be a serious and unnecessary hindrance to our understanding of human personality if we were to close our minds to the possibility of psychical transference simply because experimental science has not yet amassed sufficient data in the field. As a matter of fact, the very hypotheses science eventually proves experimentally are often truths which were stated centuries earlier by philosophers and intuitive psychologists, such as the atomic theory. The fruitful point of view is, we suggest, the frank admission that much communication and understanding occurs between persons by means subtler and more intangible than the word or gesture. This understanding in general is empathy; and the specific methods of communication, physical or psychical, are to be regarded as various aspects or instruments of empathy.

Much communication occurs between persons by means of little gestures of which they are not aware, by the almost imperceptible variations in the expression of the face, by faint winces at unpleasant thoughts and a slight lightening of the countenance at pleasing ideas. The facial expression, varying through an infinite number of nuances, reflects the inner thoughts for him who can read; and muscular activity even in the form of posture and the twitching of fingers is an expression of inner mental states. People read much more of this non-vocal expression of their fellows than they realize. Where physical transference of thought leaves off and non-physical begins we are not now in a position to state.

May I relate an experience of my own, which will be common to most people, to illustrate another approach to our question. Often when talking to another person I have a curious suspicion that he is reading more of my thoughts than I am telling him in words. With this suspicion I experience a moment of fright. Then I ask myself, why should I be afraid he will know what is going on in my mind? I proceed to remind myself that I really have nothing to keep hidden from him; he may read my thoughts if he wishes, and in fact I am quite willing to assist him with the spoken word on any matter about which he may inquire.

The point to be noticed is that by this little psychological device I am able to be more honest with the other person. I am able, that is, to give up to some extent the little game of deceit which all human beings play with each other most of the time. And I give up the deceit by the means curiously enough, of a *hypothesis of mental telepathy*, assuming that the other can read my mind and that there is therefore no point in keeping anything from him. Psychical transference thus has its ethical side in practical living. It means honesty. If people could read each other's minds, lying would be no longer possible; honesty would be not only the best but the only policy, for deception would be impossible.

The deeper one penetrates into psychological understanding, the more difficult it becomes to lie. One still tends to deceive others in such universal ways as putting his best foot forward; but psychological insight springs up at the very moment to remind him that there really is no ultimate value in always keeping the best front up. This understanding unmasks the tendencies toward self-deceit, and it discloses the real motive behind the false rationalization which one's vanity attempts. It might conceivably be true, as some uninstructed persons seem to fear, that psychological understanding would empower vicious individuals to be the more demonic and unscrupulous; for they would have learned subtler techniques of twisting others to their will. But this is mostly a bogey. On the whole it is true that understanding of depth psychology tends to remove the possibility of dishonesty and thus force one into greater honesty.

"It may cause general astonishment," writes the venerable Sigmund Freud, "to learn how much stronger is the impulse to tell the truth than is usually supposed. Perhaps it is a result of my occupation with psychoanalysis that I can scarcely lie any more." [11]

Every human being has the tendency to deceive others, because his ego is always striving to raise its own prestige at the expense of others. In so-called ethical persons this does not take the form of outright lying, but rather the form of the continuous endeavor to appear something different from, usually better than, they actually are. The purist who does not recognize his tendency to deceive others is twice-deceived—his ego has learned the game so well that it has completely deceived the man himself, and therefore has an open highway through which to deceive the world. Human motives always have more or less of the ego-bias, and this with its consequent tendency to deceive others must be recognized before one is in a position to move toward greater honesty. This is why "good" people who do not admit their evil tendencies may be more evil, as Jesus so often pointed out, than bad people who do recognize their failings.

Deceit of others and self-deceit go hand in hand. In fact if a person did not deceive himself to some degree he could not long continue to deceive others, for he would recognize the folly of the trick. Both kinds of deceit may succeed temporarily, but only to fail the more disastrously in the end, precisely because they *are deceit*. The more penetrating one's insight into the deep workings of personality, the more one is convinced of the uselessness of trying to fool either one's self or others.

Let us analyze an instance of so-called harmless deceit, the notorious and common "white lie." Mrs. Brown, say, invites Mrs. DeWitt to dinner. For some reason the latter does not wish to attend; she may send any of the stock excuses from the death of a relative to the pressure of a previous engagement. Supposing that Mrs. DeWitt is an individual without particular understanding of human nature, she will assume that Mrs. Brown has believed her white lie, and she will let the whole matter drop. We have a right to suppose, however, that Mrs. Brown suspects the other's deceit. We do not often hear of people's suspecting each other's deceit, because there are certain psychological reasons why the deceived individual does not wish to admit the fact. In this illustration Mrs. Brown would not publicly mention her suspicion; she would probably not even say anything about it to her husband; in fact, she might even refuse to admit it to herself. For entertaining the suspicion would mean recognizing that Mrs. DeWitt did not wish to dine at her house, and this would be an intolerable blow to her vanity. So she would suppress her suspicion into her subconscious; for vanity being queen, Mrs. Brown prefers to bask in her self-deceit rather than to face the truth. This suppression might come out in the form of embarrassment at her next social dinner; in any case it would not make for healthy personality.

The constructive approach Mrs. Brown should have taken would consist of the frank admission of her suspicions and an honest asking of herself the real reason underlying Mrs. DeWitt's wish to stay away. Then she would be in a position to turn her attention to correcting the mistakes which had created a disturbance in the relationship. Frankly recognizing the situation—though it would temporarily lower Mrs. Brown's "ego-prestige"—would not necessarily result in her developing an "inferiority complex"; for she would realize that all human relationships fall short of perfection and that one can best recognize this imperfection and be fitted thereby to make the relationships more nearly perfect.

Sometimes an individual is troubled by the fact that he tends, apparently without being able to prevent it, to think uncomplimentary things about the person with whom he is talking. The same process of "running the other down" is occurring on the other side, and consequently the thoughts each "reads" in the other's mind are not very palatable. Perhaps the individual will say on experiencing this, "I think so-and-so dislikes me"; but more often he will not mention his suspicion. It is best to admit the suspicion if one feels it, but as a matter of fact the mistrust is not in this case an accurate interpretation of the situation. For we have here not a matter of one person "disliking" the other, but simply the juxtaposition of egos, each of which is striving for the prestige and superiority in the relationship. It is very difficult for the ego to accept a position of inferiority. If the person actually does feel inferior, he will resort to "running the other down" in his own estimation in order to elevate himself. The more the competition, the more the jealousy or envy between two persons, the more will the one seek to push down the other. You have had the experience no doubt of suddenly realizing in the course of a conversation that you have been subconsciously asking yourself, "What can I find wrong with this person?" You were probably angry with yourself on realizing how "gossipy" you had become. But the pertinent question is, "Why should I have to disparage the other?" Which means, what inferiority feeling is there in myself that should make me strive to pull him down in order to raise myself?

Mental transference consists not only of negative, hostile ideas, but can as well carry a positive, friendly content. When talking with a loved individual, one senses affirmative, complimentary attitudes in the mind of the other. This is basic in the building up of love. People could not fall in love without making use of the process of empathy. All through history lovers have been convinced that much more communication was occurring between them than merely the spoken word or the physical expression.

Trust and confidence and other aspects of good rapport increase the effectiveness of empathy. Empathy works best of all between persons in love; here is a condition of identification of psychic states that goes on day after day, until it becomes literally impossible to draw a demarcation where the personality of one leaves off and that of the other begins. Hostility, competition, and antagonism decrease the possibilities of empathy. Continued negative attitudes make empathy, even simple understanding, finally impossible between the persons concerned. One cannot understand one's enemy so long as he is one's enemy. Thus though empathy is a means of the transfer of both hostile and friendly attitudes between people, the former breaks down the connections and progressively destroys the possibilities of empathy, while the latter increasingly strengthens the attachment. *The secret of successful personal relations is the use of empathy in this constructive, affirmative, friendly, and upbuilding form.*

90

In conclusion, may we state that the counselor and counselee may fruitfully assume that such mental transference takes place, and that there is therefore no room for anything but honesty. This means frankly that each will sense what the other is thinking, so there is no point wasting time trying to deceive each other. They can assume that their minds and hearts are as open to view as though they were placed on the table between them. This assumption means a breaking down of barriers. There is no place for pretense. The counselor then refrains from playing any little game of deceit with the counselee, and the latter realizes that he will accomplish nothing by similar devices. This is the real meaning of honesty—a demolishing of barriers until a man takes another for what he really is. It amounts, of course, to a "nakedness" in the presence of the other; but there is no more cleansing experience in the world than psychological nakedness.

And finally, this is the real meaning of sincerity—a being "without wax." It is an attitude very close, if one may say so, to what Jesus had in mind when he spoke of the single-minded, the pure in heart, and those whose answer was a simple yea or nay.

## THE SECRET OF INFLUENCE

THE DISCUSSION of empathy brings us finally to the subject of influence. This word is glibly bandied about by educators and ministers and others who realize that their aim is in the end to influence people, but rarely has the meaning of the term been given careful analysis. The popular writings on "how to influence" usually exhibit a very superficial understanding of what the process actually consists of, and thus much of their advice may be downright dangerous. Influence is a process which works chiefly in the unconscious. Better understanding of it would enable

us more to protect ourselves and others from the insidious
and vicious effects of the various waves of propaganda
which attack our civilization like diseases.

Influence is one of the results of empathy. Wherever
there is empathy some influence will be occurring, and
wherever there is influence we can expect to find some
identification of psychic states. The word has its root in
the primitive astrological idea that an "in-flowing" of
ethereal fluid from the stars affected the actions of men,
which is the early mythological recognition of the fact that
influence occurs in deep levels of the unconscious. Dic-
tionary definitions include such synonyms as "induction,"
"effusion," "emanation," all of which are definitely empathetic processes.

Let us endeavor here to analyze influence as it appears
in its different forms. There is first the *influence of ideas*.
At the beginning of a year, to cite an example, I addressed
a young people's group to which I was acting as adviser,
on a certain subject. This same subject came up again
for discussion somewhat by accident six months later. The
young people presented back ideas almost identical with
those I had suggested months earlier; they had forgotten
in the meantime the origin of the ideas and defended them
vehemently as their very own brain children. Everyone
working with people will have observed similar influence
of ideas, in which the other persons absorb the ideas and
make them their own.

A second form of influence is that which we might
term the *temporary influence of personality*. One often
notices the curious fact that two persons talking together
tend to take on the gestures, tones of voice, and general
psychic states of each other. If the one has burst into
the room heatedly and blurts out his words in an excited
voice, the other tends to take on this nervous tension.

But if the second pulls himself together, refuses to become excited and talks in a calm, leisurely manner, the first person gradually loses his nervous tension and absorbs some of this poise. The same form of influence is evidenced in the way embarrassment spreads in a social group, one embarrassed person passing on the contagion to the others until all become tense. This is all quite understandable; according to the principle of empathy it is impossible that two or more persons engage in genuine conversation without approximating each other's psychic states.

A hint for counselors arises from these observations: the skilled and sensitive counselor can put his counselee into a given mood, within certain limits, by assuming that mood himself. This is also the secret of many a successful hostess' ability to put her guests at ease.

There is thirdly a *general influence of personality*, the more permanent form of what we have described above. This occurs when one individual assumes to some extent the personality pattern or role of another. The student, for example, will take on the tone of voice or peculiar manner of gesturing of his favorite professor. Members of a church often assume the mannerisms of their minister; and whole groups will exhibit behavior patterns, oftentimes very petty and inconsequential, which they have taken on from their leader. When one meets a disciple of a certain leader, one often has an uncanny, eerie feeling on observing that some small gestures of the disciple's are actually not his own but his leader's; and one feels that it is the leader and not the disciple standing before one just as it is Hamlet and not the actor one sees on the stage. The significant point is that this influence is ordinarily unconscious, the student or the disciple not realizing that he has taken on the gesture or tone or voice of the master.

How are we to explain influence? [12] Not as the result of mere contact, like water becoming blue when ink is poured into it. To be sure, the influencing is accomplished by certain items in the individual's environment; but he *selects* these items, and by a very creative and mostly unconscious process. Since there are an infinite number of elements in every environment, an infinite number of persons can each receive a different influence from the same general environment.

Each individual, struggling as he is to attain a position of higher prestige and power, clutches at every rope in the form of a behavior pattern which gives promise of aiding him in his upward movement. He sees other individuals succeeding in their movement toward the goal he has picked for himself, and he adopts their behavior patterns by unconscious or partially conscious imitation. It is along the line of the ego's striving for power that the individual is most open to influence. It is the vain person, for example, who is attracted by the lipstick and "become-beautiful-quickly" advertisements; and the sickly child may take as his hero the policeman or the famous general who possesses the great power he desires but does not have. When one person takes another as his "ideal" we may assume that he wishes to attain the goal achieved by the other. This is a definitely emphatic process, the individual partially identifying himself with his ideal personality and thus playing the role and assuming the behavior patterns of the ideal person.

In religious and ethical education it is well to remember that the youth will not take the ideal held up before him as abstractly "good" or "recommended," but rather the one which gives the most promise of aiding him toward the position in life he wishes to attain. Under pressure he may superficially and consciously accept the ideal held up by his educators, but the ideal that deeply influences him is that which is selected by processes in his unconscious. And the assuming of a different conscious ideal may militate against the unity of his personality development and make for hypocrisy.[13]  Emphathetic identification on the part of the young person with some more ideal character is an entirely legitimate and efficacious method of ethical education, but it will come as an unconscious byproduct of the identity of goals.

Since influence is a function of the individual's struggle for prestige and power, it follows that the person who has the power in a given relationship will exert the influence.  In personal terms this power means *social courage,* which follows from such qualities as stability, maturity, and other aspects of clarification.  It is the person in a given situation with the greater social courage who exerts the influence, and the person of lesser social courage who accepts it.  Ordinarily, of course, the counselor holds the prestige by virtue of his position as well as personality, and therefore exerts the major part of the influence in the counseling situation; but if he is fatigued or for some other reason his courage is depressed, the tables may be turned.  He may find himself assuming the mood of the counselee and permitting the other to direct the interview. In such case the counselee is counseling the counselor! And the latter had best leave off the attempt to counsel until his courage has been restored.

The *truth factor* enters, of course, into any explanation of influence, particularly in respect to the influence of ideas.  If the young people in the first example above had not believed the ideas true, they would not have accepted them.  Uncritical observers, however, are inclined to overweight the truth factor, assuming that it is the only important explanation of influence; tell people the truth, they say, and that is all that is necessary.  Unfortunately our world is not so ideal. Groups are able to make themselves believe almost any piece of nonsense if it is in line with their ego-striving. Truth is still on the scaffold—witness its mutilation in European fascistic countries. The public wants to be fooled, observes Adler, whom nobody could accuse of being a cynic; and we might add that individuals allow themselves to be persuaded of an obvious untruth because it raises their prestige to believe it. It is true that the individual must believe in the truth of the idea that is influencing him, but he is able to go through a good many gymnastics of rationalization to accomplish this. *Convincingness* depends only partially, it is safe to conclude, upon the objective truth of the proposition at hand.

When we analyze a case of some pronounced influence, our question is not why the one person had the power to influence the other, but rather what tendencies were there in the mind of the other, probably in his unconscious, which made him so ready to be influenced? There must exist some unconscious readiness to believe, some predisposition toward the influence. Those who seek to protect youth from evil influences will best accomplish it not by sheltering them—this never works in our interdependent world—but rather by enabling them to achieve normal satisfactions and security in living so that they will not need to give in to the influences working on their wrong tendencies.[14]

We conclude by emphasizing several of the especially important implications for counselors. First, it is to be noticed that the *process of influence is unconscious on both sides*. The student is usually not aware that he is imitating his favorite professor's gestures and behavior patterns, and certainly the professor is not aware of it. The imitative process proceeds as part of the "*participation mystique*." It is as though the unconscious minds of the

96

one doing the influencing and the one influenced were carrying on a conversation of which their conscious minds did not know. This brings home the eternal truism that it is what the counselor really is which exerts the influence, not the relatively superficial matter of the words he utters. "What you are speaks so loudly that I cannot hear what you say."

The second implication is clear; as counselors or teachers or ministers, *we bear a tremendous responsibility*. We shall be influencing others whether they or we wish it or not, and we had best frankly recognize this. The teacher or minister is like a magnetic force on the campus or community; lines of force go out from him much farther than he ever imagines. If he is especially neurotic in tendency, he will be like the bearer of a contagious disease; and everyone in the school or community will be exposed to the infectious neurosis. But if he has become courageous and socially minded, he will be like a purifying sun; and the whole community will be disinfected and made more healthy by his cleansing rays. "All these guiding principles in therapy," Jung says in regard to the therapist, "confront the doctor with important ethical duties which can be summed up in the single rule: be the man through whom you wish to influence others." [15]

A final implication presses home: *as counselors we must learn to empathize*. This involves learning to relax, mentally and spiritually as well as physically, learning to let one's self go into the other person with a willingness to be changed in the process. It is a dying to one's self in order to live with others. It is the great giving up of one's self, losing one's own personality temporarily and then finding it a hundred fold richer in the other person. "Except a grain of wheat fall into the earth and die. . . . ."

97

*PART TWO*

PRACTICAL STEPS

*"The longer I live the more do human beings appear to be fascinating and full of interest. . . . .*

*"Foolish and clever, mean and almost saintly, diversely unhappy—they are all dear to my heart; it seems to me that I do not properly understand them and my soul is filled with an inextinguishable interest in them.  Many of them whom I knew are dead; I am afraid that except me there is no one who will tell their story as I would like to do and dare not; it will seem as though such men had never existed on earth at all. . . . .*

*"The people I am most fond of are those who are not quite achieved; who are not very wise, a little mad, 'possessed.'  'The people of a sound mind' have little interest for me.  The achieved man, the one perfect like an umbrella, does not appeal to me. I am called and doomed, you see, to describe—and what could I say of an umbrella but that it is of no worth on a sunny day?*

*"A man, slightly possessed, is not only more agreeable to me; he is altogether more plausible, more in harmony with the general tune of life, a phenomenon unfathomed yet, and fantastic, which makes it at the same time so confoundedly interesting."*

MAXIM GORKI, "Two Stories"
*The Dial,* September, 1927, pp. 197-98.

## Chapter IV

## READING CHARACTER

THE COUNSELOR's distinguishing mark is his great sensitivity to people—sensitivity to their hopes and fears and personality tensions. Particularly, the counselor is sensitive to all the little expressions of character, such as tone of voice, posture, facial expression, even dress and the apparently accidental movements of the body. And so he learns to read character—not nearly so simply as the proverbial open book, but like a traveler going through a new country, finding everything new and interesting and trying to understand.

Everything about the person adds its stroke to the painting of his personality picture. Nothing, not even the smallest movement or change in expression, is meaningless or accidental; the inner personality is continually expressing itself in voice and gesture and dress, and the only question is the counselor's ability to perceive these expressions and sense something of their meaning. The personality pattern "shows itself in an individual's every activity. It may be very obvious in his external expressions, as, for instance, the way he looks at another person, his manner of shaking hands, or of speaking. His whole personality may give an indelible impression, one way or another, which we sense almost intuitively." [1]

In this chapter we shall list a number of guiding points for the reading of character.[2] But first a caution must be stated: these expressions of character mean something slightly different with every individual, and hence the counselor should be *very tentative in drawing conclusions*. The matter is somewhat paradoxical; for though every gesture or facial expression is significant, it is the symptom —like the buoy on the water's surface—which leads in every case to a unique personality pattern, and hence the gestures and expressions of any two persons are never to be interpreted in exactly the same way.

We may here state a general caution for counselors: *hypotheses about an individual's personality pattern are to be made only from a constellation of many different factors*. Posture and tone of voice, position in the family, the particular problem the individual describes, relations to friends and to the opposite sex, success or failure in work, all of these and many more are pointer readings which indicate something, but no one in itself is sufficient basis for a conclusion. No two or three or four, in fact, are sufficient. Only when one has a number of pointer readings indicating much the same thing can one begin to set up hypotheses.

The *approach* of the counselee gives the counselor a first glimpse into his character. A firm, steady step indicates courage; whereas a hesitant step, telling that the individual has to renew his resolution at every moment, indicates timidity and a general desire to withdraw from this interview. My counseling office in a recent college position happened to be at the end of a hall, and merely hearing the student walk down this hall and knock on my door gave me an impression of what he was going to be like. One student, for example, would come a few steps down the hall, pause a moment, and then proceed a few steps further; on arriving at the door, he would knock in that apologetic way of one who hopes no one is in. Another type of student would stride down the hall, putting each foot down with a definite noise like a hero making his opening entrance on the stage, knock at the door briskly, and probably open it to enter without waiting for an invitation.

The manner of *shaking hands* has long been recognized as a significant expression of attitude and character. The "fishy" handshake, withdrawn immediately, is almost equivalent to the individual's saying, "I don't want to meet you." Such a person may act timidly toward all people, or he may simply be afraid of this particular interview. The rough, strong handshake, in which the other person grips one's hand like a vise and pumps it enthusiastically as though to impress one that he is a direct descendant of sturdy pioneer stock and in general a "he-man," may be merely an effort to compensate for some deep inferiority feeling. The handshake is a symbol of union between persons; and it is a sign of personality health when it expresses genuine friendliness, interest in the other person, and a readiness to give.

The significance of *dress* is proverbial; and human beings (perhaps we should add women in particular) have schooled themselves for many a century in reading the meaning of dress. It is not true that "clothes make the man," but it is true that details of attire give important hints about the attitudes of the person wearing the clothing. Freud explains this from the psychotherapeutic point of view: "Of equal significance to the physician and worthy of his observation, is everything that one does with his clothing, often without noticing it. Every change in the customary attire, every little negligence, such as an unfastened button, every trace of exposure means to express something that the wearer of the apparel does not wish to say directly; usually he is entirely unconscious of it." [3]

Slovenliness of dress, the need of a haircut, broken shoelaces, and so on, tell us things the meaning of which no one can mistake. On the other hand the person who is too meticulous about attire, who keeps his fingernails filed perfectly and his necktie always straight, is apt at the same time to have a too great care for details in other realms of his living. Many individuals who develop what we term in a later chapter the religious or compulsion neurosis, exhibit in their dress this exaggerated desire that everything be perfectly neat and tidy and above reproach.

The girl who paints her fingernails luridly, or the one who rouges to excess, is telling us by this means that she wants our attention. Either she does not receive enough genuine social attention or she has been pampered into demanding too much; and in either case the painting should be approached, not as an evil in itself, but as a symptom of deeper maladjustments in the girl's personality.

Counselees who are particularly anxious about the interview often pay special attention to their attire before coming. When a woman counselee, for example, arrives obviously primped for the occasion, the counselor can infer that she has been anticipating this interview and is concerned with it. Of course her primping may indicate a subjective, probably unconscious, interest in the counselor, and it then becomes even more important that he read the meaning of her careful grooming in order to guard against the subjective element in the interview. The individual who comes carelessly dressed to a party is telling us by the same token that he does not care much about the group at the party. And a habitual lack of care for one's appearance indicates a general lack of interest in other people.

Reading the meaning of *distances* is another help toward understanding individuals. If the counselee takes a chair near the counselor, we can infer a friendly attitude on his part; whereas sitting farther away indicates the existence of a barrier. This is Adler's interpretation of the meaning of distances, which I should call a sort of "geometry of love." Friendliness and interest and other aspects of love are indicated by a movement *toward*, whereas hate and the negative emotions are shown in movements *away from*. In our society, of course, persons have themselves so well under control that these movements are not at all obvious; but the counselor can observe even a slight flip of the head, or an almost imperceptible shying of one person from or toward another. The norm and ideal of personality health is in this case a free movement *toward*, the open-armed attitude toward life, or in other words, an attitude of objective love. The neurotic individual, who is always exhibiting the movement *away from*, is precisely the one who cannot love.

One way of "reading" another's thoughts is simply to observe these very slight muscular reactions to ideas that course through the person's mind. Every thought, theoretically, has its counterpart in some muscular change in the body; and if one can read these expressions—which are very simple in the matter of smiling and frowning—he has developed a capacity very useful in the understanding of other people's characters.

There are many signs by which one can observe nervousness during the interview, such as the counselee's crossing and recrossing of his legs, or grasping the arms of the chair tightly, or holding himself taut in any way. In such cases we ask ourselves, why does this individual have to be nervous; what, in other words, is he hiding or inwardly struggling with? And the answer to these questions will lead us into his personality problem.

*Facial expressions* are of course of great importance in the reading of character. Most human beings have developed the ability to read with some accuracy the meaning of the spontaneous facial expressions of their associates, but they ordinarily find it impossible to see through a feigned expression. The counselor should be able to read joy and pain and fear as expressed in a person's face; but on the other hand, he should also be able to detect pain even though the individual puts on a mask of happiness, or fear even though the other simulates poise and ease. The person who is always smiling is probably exhibiting a false optimism. Or he who is invariably perfectly poised outwardly is probably compensating for an actual fear of the situation.

I have been interested in observing the characteristics of the faces of neurotics, in photographs and in person; and I shall offer here some of my observations, which may be suggestive though they are not at all to be considered final rules. The ends of the mouth of a neurotic individual often turn down. This makes the "long" face which is the expression of pessimism, despondency, and lack of social interest. We should expect such an individual to be slow in his movements, to make negative, sarcastic comments, and to exhibit a general lack of decisiveness. The eyes of neurotics are often taut and held more widely open than normal, which is the general expression of the frightened individual. The color of many neurotics is pallid and sickly; this is quite understandable, for the neurotic attitude means a general lowering of vitality, and the person tends to become actually sick physically because of his mental turmoil. The neurotic expression seems to be very similar to the expression all of us wear in moments of great fatigue, or even fright or worry.

Dostoevski, keen student of human nature that he was, has aptly observed: "One can recognize a person's character much better by his laughter than by a boring psychological examination." [4] It is significant that the neurotic individual finds it very difficult to laugh. He can sneer or be sardonic and ironic and leer like the villains in the old-style dramas—for in these expressions, the corners of the mouth still turn *down*—but he cannot genuinely laugh. True laughter is the expression of mental health. It is an invitation to friendliness, a true proof of the open-armed attitude toward life.

The *tone of voice* can tell us much, for there is music in a voice which expresses as definite a mental and spiritual attitude as a piece of symphonic music. Oftentimes one can tell merely by the tone of voice what a speaker means even if he uses no known words. Sincerity is shown in a clear voice, courage in a steady one, and an interest in people in the voice that is so distinct that no one can escape contact with it. Certainly the individual who mouths his words or talks so quietly that you must strain to hear him does not want to make contact with you.

Nervousness and emotional turmoil are shown most clearly in the voice. If the counselee speaks slowly and with great control, like George B. in the case in the first chapter, we can infer that special psychological tensions exist in his mind. We have already noted how repressions and inhibitions can be tracked down by observing at what words the individual hesitates or gets confused or repeats himself. Or if the counselee "protests too much" we may doubt whether he actually believes what he is saying. By this overstressing of the point he gives proof of the existence in his own unconsciousness of doubts as to the truth of his statement (proof that he is trying to persuade himself as well as the listener). With his customary astuteness, Freud points out that when a writer or speaker uses an involved and round-about style, we may rightly ask what he is trying to put over on us. For honesty in speech means directness, and he who labors the point or exhibits a nervous voice or employs indirection, may be trying to attack us from the rear.

## FORGETTING AND SLIPS

IT IS NOT within our purpose to delve deeply into those most fascinating and rewarding subjects, memory and forgetting, and slips of speech and faulty actions; for the counselor does not deal directly with these expressions of his counselee's unconsciousness. But he should, however, possess some general intelligence concerning the meaning of such phenomena if he is to understand human nature at all profoundly.

One does not forget by accident. The hostess who remarks to the guest, "Oh, I'm so sorry; I forgot you were coming," or the person who pleads, "Do forgive me; I'm no good at remembering names," are begging forgiveness actually under false pretenses; and the guest and the person whose name is forgotten are right in being somewhat offended. For memory works with a purpose. Within the unconsciousness of the individual a selective process goes on which sorts out those things desired to be remembered prominently and puts away other things. Nothing, it is probably safe to say, is ever really forgotten. Our problem, then, is why certain things are tossed to the forefront of the mind, while others are pushed so far back that the individual can recall them only with effort or perhaps not at all.

In his earliest work Freud noticed this curious purposiveness in forgetting. He interpreted it in terms of the pleasure-pain sifting, concluding that the individual forgets those things which are associated with something unpleasant in his experience. Thus the mechanism of forgetting gave Freud an entrance to the understanding of the unconscious. But Freud's explanation is incomplete; for often we remember most vividly precisely those experiences which caused us most pain, such as a humiliating and embarrassing social *faux pas*. And so Adler went deeper by pointing out that the individual remembers those experiences which have a special significance for his style of life.[5] Out of this insight Adler developed one of his most useful contributions to psychotherapeutic analysis—his famous use of the *early childhood memory* as an avenue to the understanding of the style of life [6] of the person. We may explain this as follows: a thousand things happened to John Doe, let us say in his third or fourth year of infancy, but he forgot all the other experiences and remembered this one. Why should this one image be selected in his unconsciousness and hung up like a guidepost in the forefront of his memory all these years? Clearly this early childhood memory must possess some peculiar significance, and it possesses this significance regardless of whether it is a true happening or an imagined one. Adler concluded that such an early memory is a little close-up snapshot, if rightly interpreted, of the individual's personality pattern.

This theory turns out to be true practically as well as theoretically, for very often we can see in the early memory the same general tendencies which the personality pattern of the individual manifests twenty years later. The understanding of the early memories can be of value to counselors, as will be pointed out in the next chapter, given sufficient tentativeness and caution in interpretation.

Slips of speech and faulty actions, like memory and forgetting, are expressions of the unconsciousness of the individual. In these phenomena the unconscious material springs into expression in spite of the conscious censorship; it gets by the watchdog in a sudden leap. It has become common banter nowadays to interpret one's companion's slips of speech, and to amuse a parlor group by "psycho-scandalizing" people on the basis of these slips. The interpretations given in this bantering are apt to be wrong, but the underlying theory—namely, that a slip in speech actually says what one really is thinking but did not intend to say—is quite accurate. We have all had experiences similar to that of a friend of mine who was introducing a line of sorority girls to a very notable person when one approached bedecked in an impossibly large hat; my friend, much to her horror and the amusement of the group, introduced her as "Miss Hat."

One could recount such stories endlessly; but we shall merely point out the basic consideration, that all slips of speech and faulty actions are to be viewed as having a meaning even though that meaning may be too recondite for the uninitiated to discover. The boy loses his school books, but not his fishing equipment. The student forgets his appointment with the professor, but his date with the new blonde sophomore, never! The housewife who is constantly misplacing or losing her keys, it has been aptly observed, has never become reconciled to the position of being a housewife.[7]

The interpretation of some phenomena in this field is not particularly difficult, and in such cases the counselor can justifiably use his observations. For example, if an individual is continually tardy for appointments or forgets them entirely, we are justified in hypothesizing that in his unconsciousness there exists an attitude of hesitancy, a

110

tendency to withdraw from the subject in question. Or if a person continually forgets names, we may rightly infer that he lacks adequate social interest. The common remark, "I've never been any good at remembering names," might be translated into the more truthful, "I'm not particularly interested in people." In all of these generalizations there will appear many exceptions; but the generalization possesses some validity nevertheless, and will be useful to the skilful and cautious counselor.

The reader who wishes to delve more deeply into this most fascinating area of memory and slips and faulty actions will find an abundance of material.[8] Here let us merely point out that though the counselor does not use these phenomena like the psychotherapist as means of prying into the unconsciousness of the individual, he may with great profit aim to be intelligent about their meaning and thus increase his general understanding of human nature. Sometimes he will be able to interpret this meaning, more often not. In this realm he is interested in *observing intelligently* rather than in drawing conclusions.

### THE FAMILY CONSTELLATION

WE HAVE another valuable guide to the understanding of an individual's personality pattern, namely, the position in his family in which he grew up. It is quite understandable that this family position should be very significant; for the person spends his first years, the most formative ones, almost entirely at the mercy of his family. The main lines of his personality pattern are laid down very early in life, some psychologists say as early as the third year of infancy; and later character depends on the way he uses this original pattern. In our endeavor to understand any person it is therefore essential that we look to his position in the family constellation.

Fortunately we are able to discover some general tendencies connected with certain positions in the family constellation.[9] The *oldest child* in a family tends to have a prominent sense of responsibility. He has enjoyed the entire love and solicitude of his parents during his first years, and this has lent him a certain stability. He also has been entrusted with responsibility from his earliest days, probably having been called upon to help the mother in little tasks and even in the bringing up of the other children. He has likely been the recipient of the parents' confidences and a sharer in their planning to a much greater degree than the other children. The oldest child thus tends to uphold law and order, to be conservative and a lover of stability. We may think of him allegorically as trying to get back to that original state of the first years of infancy when he was the king, sitting alone on the throne of his parents' affections.

This favored position of the eldest has long been recognized in folk customs in the tradition of passing the crown or the aristocratic title or even the peasant's plot of land down to the eldest son. Mrs. D., the oldest of five children, illustrates the characteristics of this position in the family. One of her earliest memories was assisting her mother in the household duties by picking up the paper. She used to help regularly in the care of the younger children, and her mother shared her plans with her even from a very early age. Now Mrs. D. occupies a position entailing considerable responsibility, and discharges her duties very creditably.

We find quite different tendencies in the *second child*. When he comes into the world he is confronted by a rival who is already one or two years old. Through his infancy and childhood he has always had this pace-setter ahead of him, who is able to walk and talk and do many things before he can. The second child thus has his inferiority held up before him vividly and continuously. And so he extends himself like a racer trying to overtake the pace-setter. But as fate has decreed it the other child always has the advantage in growth and size, and the probability is that no matter how hard the second strives he will not be able to catch up. He may seize upon a special realm of activity in which he can better the elder. The situation is complicated, also, by the fact that the elder may become jealous of the second, regarding him as an upstart who came to dethrone him in his parent's affections. All of these attitudes are deeply buried in the unconsciousness, of course; and oftentimes the individual himself will never admit this rivalry with his brother or sister even though objective signs indicate it clearly.

The second child, then, tends to develop an exaggerated ambition and the habit of striving at a great tension. He tends also to be the revolutionary; his early situation was not of the best, and we can picture him, again allegorically, as desirous of upsetting the applecart and starting things off again on a more even footing. The counselor often encounters vivid examples of this inferiority-ambition pattern of the second child. George B., the tremendously ambitious reformer of the case study in chapter one, was, we remember, the second child following a girl, which makes the situation more serious because girls develop physically more quickly than boys in the early years.

Those between the second and the youngest child occupy positions which are less significant, and there is little that can be predicted about them. But the *youngest child* has been recognized all through history as standing in a special position. In many fairy tales it is the youngest daughter who marries the prince, or the youngest son who by unusual ability achieves greatness and becomes the savior of the whole family.

This youngest child has ordinarily been the recipient of an unusual amount of affection during his infancy and youth, not only from his parents but from his older brothers and sisters as well. All these grown-ups have helped him, done things for him, taken care of him and no doubt endeavored to instruct and educate him. This may give the youngest child a particularly affectionate attitude toward the world and a general expectancy that he will love and be loved by everybody. We all know youngest children who are extraordinarily likable. But the danger is that he become especially pampered, and consequently expect the world always to coddle and comfort him. And when he finds it does not, he may take on a neglected and pouting attitude. Miss R., an example of the youngest child, was a person of unusual charm and attractiveness. But her personality difficulty lay in her expectation that the world be too beautiful, good, and ideal; and she tended to become cynical and distrustful when her hopes were disappointed.

The youngest child may, on the other hand, interpret his situation as one of inferiority, since his world is made up of powerful adults; and he may consequently develop a strong ambition and vow that when he grows up he will surpass all the others.

And now concerning the *only child*. People have recognized for ages how difficult was this position. The entire love and solicitude of the parents have been heaped upon this child; they have been particularly watchful lest anything happen to this, their only baby; and the child thus receives much more attention and educative effort than children who have brothers and sisters. This only child, too, does not have the experience of social contacts, of learning to live with other individuals, which children of larger families receive. All of this means that this child has the most likelihood of being pampered and thereby developing a demanding and dependent attitude toward life. He may expect the world to come to him, as indeed his infant's world did. And when it does not, he may secretly feel he has been betrayed, and take on a resentful and uncourageous attitude toward life.

The picture facing the only child is not, however, entirely black. He has greater possibilities for development than other children; for he has been the recipient of the combined educative efforts of both his parents, and he will have had more opportunities for self-development. Greater dangers, in the case of the only child as in all personality development, go hand in hand with greater possibilities.

Miss Helen M. was an only child. Until she was twenty-seven her parents had made most of her decisions. Her father had showered her with affection, but had been dominating at the same time; and her earliest memory was of his spanking her all the way home after she had got lost. We note here a mistake that parents often make—that of bestowing unusual affection on the child and yet disciplining it severely at the same time, both of which tend to spoil it. Such parents are especially strict and severe with the child because they see the danger in their loving it too much, then return to it with great affection to balance their disciplining, and so on until the poor child does not know what to make of his strange world. When Miss Helen M. went away to college she was troubled by an oppressive inferiority feeling although she was actually very attractive. We observe here that the inferiority feeling is not an index of one's actual inferiority, but a special interpretation the individual makes of his situation; in many cases it is merely a technique by which one separates one's self from one's social group. Miss M. had difficulty making contacts with other students on the campus, and consequently kept up her practice of running home frequently. After graduation she obtained a teaching job; but such was the strain of this situation where she had to be independent and make decisions for herself that, even though she lived at home, she suffered long weeping spells, often could not go to sleep at night, and was on the verge of a nervous breakdown. At the time of this counseling she was twenty-eight, unmarried, and not even in love. The superficial observer, noticing her attractiveness, would be surprised at this. But the more profound student of human nature knows that courage and the ability to make important decisions are prerequisite even to falling genuinely in love, let alone getting married; and the pampered child lacks these qualities. Miss M. reported that she had been "sublimating" her sexual instinct—which, as we shall discuss in a later chapter, is a common means of escaping responsibility for solving one's sexual problem. She was a very intelligent woman, however; and through her understanding of herself and her situation, we can expect that she will be able to develop the necessary courage and independence, and thus put her talents and capabilities to socially constructive work and at the same time solve the problem of her love life creatively.

Other positions in the family constellation, we shall remark in conclusion, have particular effects upon the individual. Twins, for example, often tend to develop in opposition to each other, each choosing different lines in which to specialize and surpass. A boy growing up in a family of girls will exhibit certain tendencies, as will a girl born into a family of boys. Sometimes the counselor can obtain valuable hints by discovering which members of the family the counselee was most attached to and those with whom he did not get along.

By understanding the family background we are able to see the counselee's character in perspective. We see the road down which he has traveled, and thus we are much better able to understand his condition when he reaches us. The direction in which he is moving then becomes clearer to us; and this movement is the concern, in our dynamic understanding of personality, which is of most interest. Sometimes when counseling I get sudden glimpses of this person at six or ten or twenty, almost as vividly as if he were to be transformed into his boyhood form for a moment before me. As counselor I never permit myself to set up any hypotheses about an individual until I know his background; in fact one could not, for it is like trying to solve an equation with one number missing. In cases where this background cannot be ascertained—as when one conjectures about the weary person sitting opposite him on a streetcar—one finds one's self automatically hypothesizing an imaginary background.

It should remain clear that the family background is not to be thought of as a total *cause* of the individual's present situation. We must not slip into an easy determinism at this point. A counselee may try to blame his present difficulty on something in his childhood environment, but to the extent that he thinks of himself still as a product of cause and effect his re-adjustment of personality will be thwarted. It is the counselor's function—after admitting all the force of the childhood environment, and in fact pointing out to the counselee many aspects of this influence which he had not suspected—to indicate insistently that the present concern is how this background is to be *used* for the most creative adjustment. Granted that the eldest tends to be conservative; there is no limit to the socially constructive use to which this tendency, in the form of social responsibility, can be put. And granted that the second tends to be revolutionary; many of society's greatest benefactors, and individuals who achieved a very creative adjustment of their personality tensions, have been reformers who turned their ambitions to the service of humanity. The individual's background is an aid to understanding, but not a total explanation. The locus of the personality problem still remains within the inmost area of the individual's free creativity.

As you have been reading this chapter, you have no doubt been feeling that many of the observations were far-fetched and possibly even a little dangerous. So we shall conclude as we began, with the caution that hypotheses about an individual's personality pattern are to be drawn only from a constellation of many different factors. All the considerations we have been describing—the counselee's posture, his manner of speaking, his family position, his early childhood memory, what he now forgets or the slips in speech he commits, the nature of his present problem—all of these tell something to the alert counselor. When a majority of these pointer readings indicate the same thing, the counselor can begin to set up a hypothesis, but not before. We use the term "hypothesis" advisedly, because one never draws final conclusions when dealing with a personality; the material is not that static. I have found it advisable to juggle the observations about in my mind, putting off the forming of a hypothesis until suddenly the facts fall into line as though by themselves.

The purpose of this chapter has been to sensitize the counselor. We do not wish to outfit him with a set of rules —heaven forbid! We wish rather to help him to become alert to the infinite number of ways of "feeling out" character, and to render him so sensitive to people that this reading—shall we say *appreciating*—of their characters becomes second nature. To every generalization offered above there are all kinds of exceptions; our discussion has aimed to suggest and stimulate rather than to codify. And there are thousands of ways of understanding character which we have not even touched upon. It is our hope that the counselor will endeavor to explore these ways by himself. To understand people—that is the counselor's job.

Is there danger in this emphasis upon reading other peoples' character? Will they object, as is sometimes argued, if you continually "study" them? Of course—if you go about it like one peeking into another's private room. This sort of "analysis" is directly opposite to what we have been talking about; it is actually done because the analyst wishes to set himself above other people by means of "getting their number." The true counselor goes at it altogether differently. He seeks to understand people from the standpoint of appreciation. And far from objecting, people prize this kind of understanding. For it raises the prestige of the one who is understood, and helps give him a sense of his worth as a person. This understanding breaks down the barriers which separate a man from his fellows; it draws the other human being for a moment out of the loneliness of his individual existence and welcomes him into community with another soul. It is like inviting the traveler in from his snowy and chilly journey to warm himself for an hour before the fire on another's hearth. Such understanding, it is not too much to say, is the most objective form of love. That is why there is always a tendency on the part of the counselee to feel some love toward the counselor, this person "who understands me." There are few gifts that one person can give to another in this world as rich as understanding.

*Chapter V*

## SETTING UP A COUNSELING PROGRAM

GENERALLY SPEAKING, counseling is done everywhere. At a football game, on the street car, during an evening walk across the campus after a committee meeting—in short, everywhere that people meet. For in every human contact some molding of personality occurs, and this, after all, is the fruit of counseling. We could state this definition: *personal counseling is any deep understanding between persons which results in the changing of personality.* Thus counseling is a matter of degree, and one cannot strictly classify some relationships as counseling and others as not. It is not an eight-hour-a-day job, not an activity that one performs in his office and then leaves as a carpenter does his tools when the whistle blows.

But it is still true that setting up a specific counseling program in terms of offices and hours will serve to direct this counseling attitude into its most fruitful channels. We therefore shall describe here some aspects of specific counseling programs which are already established in various institutions and could serve as models for programs in other institutions. The particular form of program depends always on the local situation, of course; and so what follows is to be treated as suggestive rather than ready-made or exhaustive.

Let us first consider *educational situations.* Every college has certain administrative officers, such as deans or personnel directors, whose job consists to a great extent of specific counseling. The good dean or personnel officer, from this point of view, is not only one who possesses the ability to gain *and* hold the confidence of students—which is a *sine quo non*, but one who also knows and can apply the underlying principles of counseling in order to avoid both the Scylla of being merely an "advice-giver" and the Charybdis of being only a likable fellow.

Many educational institutions have a corps of picked faculty members, serving under the leadership of one of these administrative officers, as "student advisers" or "freshman advisers." This is theoretically an excellent system. If perfected, it would be one of the most effective means of handling the problem of counseling students. But in practice it often falls woefully short of its possibilities because, first, the faculty participants do not have adequate time to give to student interviews. It is only fair, and certainly expedient, that their curricular and other academic burdens be sufficiently lightened to allow them this necessary time. And in the second place, it is essential, if this system is to work effectively, that the faculty members be given some training in counseling principles; for a simple desire to help, even though very valuable, does not make one able to meet the situation. Some colleges solve this problem by having a specialist in counseling come to the campus and lead several training meetings of the faculty advisers. If this is not practicable, it will be possible in some cases to hold such training meetings under the leadership of members of the college psychology and sociology departments.

Occasionally favored institutions have a trained counselor or psychological consultant on the staff, who, in addition possibly to other duties devotes himself directly to the promoting of personality health among students.

This is almost the ideal. The time will no doubt come when every university of pretensions will have such a staff member. For in our student groups, it may as well be admitted, we are continually confronted by individuals who need specific psychological help, and that in more concentrated fashion than the dean or faculty advisor is able to give. High intellectual development, a tendency to separate thought from experience, the sex problem accentuated by a postponement of marriage, all the adjustments connected with maturation—these features and others of the typical campus increase the neurosis potential and make personality problems more to be expected. An educational institution could thus perform a most valuable service to its students by placing on its staff a counselor whose purpose it would be not only to help students meet specific difficulties but to assist them in every way to adjust their personalities more creatively.

There is a caution to be added however. The work of this counselor or psychological consultant should not be such as to be branded on the campus as "pathological." The apprehension sometimes expressed that having a strictly psychiatric emphasis on the campus might create problems in addition to solving them is well founded. If a student has definite psychotic tendencies, he should be referred to a practicing psychiatrist. But the chief emphasis of the counselor should be on personality health, and he should be considered by students as a positive influence on the campus rather than one who deals merely in ill health. Giving the counselor some other functions in the college program, such as the teaching of one course, often helps in establishing this desired reputation.

Almost every professor, quite apart from his "adviser" status, is called upon to act the role of counselor dozens of times a week. Students' curricular problems, and social, economic, and even sex and matrimonial problems often fall into his lap. Thus a great opportunity for significant help is open to the professor who has the counseling attitude and knows something of basic counseling principles.

The counseling approach is of great value in the classroom. In fact the whole teaching procedure, it can be asserted, is most effective when approached with an understanding of personality and its empathetic functions. Significant teaching requires empathy, for only thus does the professor's mind meet the student's in a fructifying intellectual experience. The teacher without empathy is like a motor car with the gears unmeshed—the motor races, making a noise as ineffectual as "sounding brass and a clanging cymbal." Knowledge may go from mind to mind through relatively impersonal means; but we should all admit that the more significant kind of knowledge is that in which there is a mutual participation, a partial identification of the minds of teacher and student. Then truth is made a living force passed from one to another, and education becomes truly a "leading out" of the highest creative potentialities of the student's mind through inspiring contact and participation in the creative actualities of the teacher's mind.

The *minister* has a somewhat different situation in regard to the setting up of a counseling program, and in some ways even more favorable. He has an entree into the hearths of many families, and is, practically as well as ideally, the confidant of persons of all ages. The sensitive minister can make the pastoral visit an excellent opportunity for specific counseling. But he will need here so to direct the conversation that it not be wasted on incidentals but pierce to the heart of the problems of the individuals concerned. The pastoral visit can lead to individuals calling on the minister with their problems, which is a more advantageous setup for counseling.

The minister has the opportunity, also, to mold empathetically the personalities of his congregation in his sermons. A sermon working on the principle of empathy is one which is so filled with understanding of the people concerned that it moves into their minds and hearts and *lifts* them rather than driving them by exhortation. It is not like a proclamation nanded down from above, which anyone may take or leave; it is, if one may say so, a sort of rising of the minister and people all together. The truth the minister thus expresses is fructifying, and the people reach out for it because it represents their highest and deepest yearnings. In this case the seeds are sown on fertile ground because the sensitive preacher so well understands the people to whom he ministers. Ideally, the members of the congregation should have in the church service much the same experience as the individual has in the counseling interview; they should go out from church having experienced a psychological and spiritual catharsis, and feeling enlightened, encouraged, and strengthened by their new understanding of reality.

The student religious workers, such as student pastors and directors of student Christian associations, represent a still different type of situation. Though they have other duties they seek to reserve time for specific counseling as one of the most significant aspects of their work. In the rest of the discussion in this chapter we shall speak directly about the student worker's situation, although the suggestions will be applicable to faculty and ministerial counseling as well.

## MAKING CONTACTS

MANY COUNSELORS find their chief problem at the outset

the getting into contact with the individuals who need counseling help. These are often precisely the persons who do not simply "happen in." There are a number of ways of managing this making of contacts, and each counselor will need to find those best suited to his situation. I have found it useful to make an announcement that one has certain "counseling hours" in which he will be in the office accessible to all who wish to consult him. This puts a professional touch to the matter and disseminates the idea that one is prepared to do counseling. The student director, for example, may have a short article run in the college paper announcing his counseling hours and mentioning that he is trained in counseling. And he may have faculty members suggest to students with personality difficulties that they interview him. Such publicity should be unassuming and without fanfare. One's reputation as a counselor grows on the basis of the fruits of his work, not on the loudness of the blowing of trumpets.

The most significant advertising that a counselor may receive is by *word of mouth* of those he has counseled. One student will say to another "Mr. C. helped me a lot. You should go in and see him." This means that it may take a relatively long time for a counseling program to get under way, a matter of months or possibly even a year. A student worker or minister who comes into a new situation should not be disappointed if it takes the entire first year so to convince people of his integrity and understanding that individuals who need help will come regularly to him.

There are certain more arbitrary methods of making contacts. Interviewing about jobs or class schedules or business matters may lead to the individual's returning later with a specific personality problem. At a college where I was directing student religious work, I instituted a system of interviewing every fifth man on the campus to get information regarding campus attitudes, and the openings for personal counseling that resulted were unlimited. This proved also an excellent method of getting information about the student body as a whole, which served as a very useful background in counseling individual students. But .the student's autonomy should be respected; if the counselor has asked the student for an interview to give him ininformation, he should not suddenly turn the tables by becoming adviser.

The counselor should exhibit a *readiness to be seen*, but not appear *too eager*. After a speech he may be approached by a student with a question on some problem; and he may well let fall the invitation, "I'd be glad to have you drop into my office to talk further about that." But if the counselor is so eager that he rushes ahead and sets the appointment, the student will feel that he is making the call on the counselor's initiative, not his own. We can never ask another to come in to talk about his problems; this violates the autonomy of personality. And it would ruin the interview before it even started, for the transformation of personality occurs only when the individual himself is in readiness for it. We may suggest his coming in, to be sure, or when a third person mentions the personality problem of another, we can ask him to suggest to this other that he make an appointment. But it must be arranged that the immediate initiative come always from the counselee rather than the counselor.

The *place* in which the interviews are held should be attractive and free from interruption. Furnishings, pictures, and flowers can be utilized in the establishing of the harmonious, peaceful atmosphere which will make possible intimate conversation. This place, be it one's office or a room set aside for counseling, should be accessible but at the same time sufficiently off the beaten path to be protected from disturbance. One cannot do significant counseling with other persons bobbing in and out of the room continually, or with the phone ringing and breaking the counselee's line of thought. It has been my practice to take the counselee out of my office into a side room for the period of the interview. However, it is advisable to avoid creating an atmosphere of great secrecy by shutting one's self behind too many closed doors; the counselee should feel that it is a private but not a secret and solemn occasion. That is why taking the counselee for a walk, and thus giving the interview a certain romantic touch, often does not contribute to the most objective interviewing. For the same reason it is often preferable to use one's office or special room for interviews, other things being equal, than one's home, for the subjective touch of hospitality may militate against the calm, business-like objectivity of the counseling interview.

## ESTABLISHING RAPPORT

COMING NOW to the conduct of the counseling interview itself, we find our first concern the establishing of rapport with the counselee. The shaking of hands can be an excellent beginning of this; it can convince the other person of warm, genuine friendliness and be an effective first step in a growing empathy. Rapport depends on each person's being at ease, and the best way to assist the counselee in this regard is for the counselor to be at ease himself and show it. Let both counselee and counselor sit comfortably, so that there will be as little artificial tension as possible One cannot over-emphasize the psychological importance of relaxation: artificial tension is always symptomatic of barriers or dams to psychic activity. Relaxation undermines the dam so that the stream of empathy can break it down and flow through. We could say, parenthetically, that the ability to relax is one of the surest symptoms of mental health. The neurotic must live at a tension like a gangster tracked by the police, for his unsolved problems of life relentlessly haunt him.

In his attitude toward the other person at the beginning of the interview, the counselor must *balance sensitivity and robustness*. The meaning of sensitivity in this regard is understood by all, and hence the particular danger is in going too far—letting one's sensitivity appear too obvious. The moment the counselor becomes "delicate" or "precious," the counselee will feel him ungenuine and proceed to withhold some of his confidence. Here we see the need of *robustness*, a quality aided by a hearty voice and a good sense of humor. This tension between sensitivity and robustness is not easy to establish; and it varies, of course, with the persons concerned. Paradoxically, one must be sensitive enough to know when to be robust.

The chief barrier to establishing rapport is the *professional manner*. If the dean greets the student perfunctorily and then settles back in his chair in a way that speaks more loudly than words, "I'm the dean, and this is just another case for me," the interview is strangled before it begins. Or if the pastor exhibits the ministerial manner or voice, rapport will be made very difficult. Every profession has its trade-mark, to be sure, and one accepts the mark with the trade. The important point is that in counseling the counselor must be a human being before he is a dean or a minister or anything vocational; and his tone of voice, his whole attitude should be that of a fellow human being.

In work with students I have encountered a very definite prejudice against the ministerial manner. Students point out this manner as exhibited in a sonorous tone of voice, a forced sense of humor, or back-slapping and effusive friendliness. The "parsonal" is here the enemy of the

128

"personal." One can certainly be a man as well as a minister, and it is the man that counts in counseling.

Our final principle in the matter of establishing rapport concerns the *ability to use the other person's language.* Language is the ordinary channel of empathy, and two persons who have progressed to some degree of personal identification will find themselves automatically employing a common mode of speech. In fact, one could measure the degree of empathy of the minister with his people or the teacher with his students by their ability to speak the others' language.

While living among various peoples in Europe, I observed that when the other person, say my French companion, translated himself into English to facilitate my understanding, I found my empathy with him only slight. He was, so to speak, coming to me. But when I translated myself into Greek to converse with peasants in the villages of Greece, I experienced a pronounced empathy with them. The conclusion is that one can best identify himself with another by using the language of the other. We know from experience that the professor who speaks forever in a sociological or over-precise language has a difficult time getting close to students. If the student remarks as they walk down the street, "Gosh, what a rain!" and the professor answers, "Indeed, it is undoubtably the most disagreeable precipitation of the season," the barriers to empathy become temporarily insurmountable.

For the university pastor, this speaking the student's language means the occasional use of so-called slang. Frequently these expressions carry great power—and that, in the end, is the criterion of effective language. The expression, "He's got the stuff," for example, means something to students that it would take paragraphs to define, and then one would have killed the meaning anyway. Or the more sarcastic expression, "So what?" has a particularly powerful meaning, or "He's got something on the ball," or any one of the many campus expressions.

This using of slang expressions is not necessarily the contradiction of distinguished English. Both choice English and slang carry their power, and the most effective student workers are those who can employ both. Their speech then has a flexible, motile, warm and human quality.

The readers of this book will have, in all probability, a prejudice against the use of slang. We are the linguistic pharisees who have a certain deep feeling about "proper" and "improper" words, slang being relegated without reprieve to the latter category. But this very concern for detailed correctness in language can be a barrier to empathy. A formal language has a tendency to separate one from real life like any other formalization. This exaggerated concern for correctness can be classed as an embryonic compulsion neurosis. We know certainly that the use of highly grammatical language is for some people a way of elevating themselves over other human beings whose language is not so correct.

It is—if the caution be necessary—unfortunate when the professor or minister "bends over backwards" to use the expressions of the street. We have all smiled to ourselves at the alumnus who acts more fresh than the freshmen or the father who endeavors to be younger than his son. All of this is not what we are talking about; this is actually ungenuine, and a product of the individual's egoistic striving for recognition rather than true empathy.

Empathy means the mutual influence of personalities; and therefore in the process of empathy not only will the student counselor take on the powerful expressions of the students, but they, in their turn, will absorb his larger and more carefully chosen vocabulary.

## Chapter VI

## CONFESSION AND INTERPRETATION

CONTACT having been made with the counselee, and rapport having been established, we now find ourselves in the central stage of the interview, the *confession*. This stage consists of the counselee's "talking it out." It is the *piece de resistance* of both counseling and psychotherapy. So important, in fact, is the confession that counselors can well hold themselves to the practice initiated by the psychotherapists; namely, that of reserving at least two-thirds of every hour for talking on the part of the counselee.

After the counselee has talked out his problem, described his situation, and laid all his cards on the table, the *interpretation* stage takes place. During this period both counselee and counselor survey the facts that have been brought to light and endeavor to discover through them the personality pattern of the counselee, wherein lie the sources of his maladjustment. Interpretation is a function of both counselor and counselee working together. In the confession stage the counselee occupies the limelight and does practically all the talking. But in the interpretation the counselor becomes increasingly prominent, first merely by asking leading questions, then by offering suggestive insights, and finally, by his empathetic influence upon the counselee.

Probably the most fruitful approach will be to illustrate the confession and interpretation stages by narrating an actual interview. I shall therefore describe a two-hour interview, in condensed form, using as much as possible the exact words of the counselee and counselor. This case is selected because the counselee in question was particularly intelligent, and therefore the interpretation could proceed without waste of time. But for that very reason the case is not to be regarded as typical, for most counselees will require a much slower process. At the end of the narration we shall sum up and examine the more important points emerging in the interview.

Mr. Bronson, as we shall term our counselee, was a college instructor in philosophy of religion. When he came for counseling I noticed that he was an attractive, intelligent-appearing young man. He shook my hand cordially and exhibited a very friendly attitude. We exchanged a few sentences and then without the customary procrastination, Mr. Bronson went immediately into his problem.

Bronson: I am troubled by the fact that I always work at a great tension. I can't seem to relax. When I let up at all, I get sick. It's rather strange—the second day of every vacation I feel myself all done out, and have to go to bed with a cold or something of the sort. (*He laughs.*)

Counselor: Well, that's interesting. Tell me more about it.

Bronson: It seems as though I must always have something driving me, something compelling me to keep at my work. If I don't have this strong outside compulsion, I just slump altogether.

Counselor: You mean driving you in your teaching?

Bronson: Yes, but also in other aspects of my work, such as writing articles. When I have to write a book review, for example. I read the book, make a *precis* of it, fuss over it, throw myself into the writing; and then after spending a lot of time on it I put it away and never finish it. As a matter of fact, I must have a dozen unfinished articles lying around my office, which I have never used.

Counselor: Yes, you do appear to work at a great strain. How long have you noticed this tension?

*(By this time the counselor has observed some of the external manifestations of the counselee's character. Mr. Bronson sits in a friendly manner, not appearing at all hostile. But his movements are jerky and definitely nervous, and from time to time he pulls one leg up and sits on it in a taut position. His eyes have a somewhat faded and fatigued appearance, and his complexion is pallid.)*

Bronson: Always. At least, ever since I can remember. In high school I worked very hard and fast—I was quite small then, only four feet ten; and I had to use my brains to get what I wanted. So I did good work scholastically. Then when I went on to college, I continued to work at the same tension and have kept it up ever since. I've always had something of an economic problem, which didn't help matters.

Counselor: Tell me more about how this tension appears in your living now.

Bronson: The main trouble is that I cannot get accomplished what I want to. When I have to do something, such as correcting papers, I put it off and pick up something else which is more interesting. And finally, when the last moment comes, I throw myself into the work with great fury and get it done in a burst of speed. I work in this tense manner on articles, too; but with them I feel I always must do a little more, read another book or two, or rewrite the article because it isn't perfect; and consequently I never get it finished.

Counselor: But have you never thought that you could

do better creative work if you did not keep yourself at this great tension?

Bronson: Yes, I have realized that often. But at other times I feel that I must have something compelling me from the outside. I have a great horror of ever getting into a position where I would not have these external drives, for then I would go to seed immediately. I feel I do better teaching when I throw myself into it with great energy.

*(We note here an inconsistency in the counselee's thought; he complains that working at the great strain causes his difficulties, yet he feels that the outside compulsions are useful, and he appears desirous of retaining them. This inconsistency shows us that the tensions of which he complains are really symptoms of some maladjustment deeper in his personality. His statement that he works better under strain is not to be taken at its face value, for he would be forced to rationalize the matter in some such way as this.)*

But it's pretty hard on me. The night before I gave my first lecture in philosophy I didn't sleep a wink. And it was the same the night before I substituted for Professor Brown in his lecture; and I was terribly nervous and upset in the class even though I knew all the students.

*(We observe from the material so far that Mr. Bronson is not particularly abnormal. He occupies a good position and is what the world calls a successful young man. But he is potentially neurotic and could slip into neurosis at any time the pressure was sufficient, as we shall see below. More important, we notice that his personality difficulty is distinctly inhibiting his creative accomplishment. In this respect he clearly needs to be "liberated." The counselor's purpose in this case, then, is to help Mr. Bronson*

134

*to readjust his personality tensions so that first, the possibility of his going neurotic in the future will be lowered, and second, his creative powers will be freed.)*

Counselor: Have you ever had a breakdown under these strains?

Bronson: Yes, when I was a senior in college I had a nervous collapse. I had just got engaged, and that made me strive all the harder. Suddenly I went off into a sort of dreamy state—I couldn't study, couldn't do anything. They sent me with my sister down to the ocean, where we stayed for three months. I was in a comatic state; I went to sleep, woke up, but did practically nothing else. But finally I came back to college and finished out the year. Another time . . . . (*Here Mr. Bronson begins to laugh.*) Once I had a terrible time. I was phoned one night to take a fairly important Bible class on the following morning. I didn't know much about the subject, but I couldn't get out of it. I stayed up all night, all my muscles taut and my body as nervous as could be, drinking coffee and trying to look over some notes. But I got nothing done. Next morning I got on the bus in a fuddle, scarcely knowing what I was doing. I felt a strange pain at the base of my brain, as though something were going wrong. While riding the bus I looked across at the Jersey shore and felt a strong desire—(*he emphasizes the point,*) honestly, a pull that was almost too strong to be resisted, to take the train to Jersey and escape the whole thing.

Counselor: (*laughing*) Well, you did get pretty close to the line.

Bronson: (*also laughing*) Yes, I know that's the way people go crazy—if I'd waked up in California and not known how I got there, they'd have locked me up in the asylum for sure. But I didn't go to Jersey. When I got to the class I saw it consisted of a bunch of old ladies whom nobody should be afraid of, and so I walked in and got off some old drivel. But, boy, that was an experience!

(*So far the interview consists entirely of confession, the counselee merely "talking it out." This goes on much longer than is here recorded. Now the counselor must elicit certain necessary information from the counselee.*)

Counselor: What is your age, Mr. Bronson? And tell me something, if you will, about your family and your position in it.

Bronson: I am twenty-six. I am the second child in our family, my sister being two years older. My father is a minister.

(*The counselee also gives the information that he married at twenty and has had entirely happy relations with his wife. Evidently the sex factor does not play a prominent role in this maladjustment.*)

Counselor: You appear to have a tremendously strong ambition. (*This marks the beginning of the stage of interpretation. The counselor will now seek to point out various relationships in the personality in the endeavor to find the underlying pattern.*)

Bronson: Yes, I am very ambitious. I have always worked very hard to succeed.

Counselor: Now we know that an exaggerated ambition, when the individual is not able to let up his striving, is very often connected with some deep inferiority feeling . . . .

Bronson: (*interrupting*) I certainly have had an inferiority complex. It was connected with my being so small in high school, and I had to strive hard to make a place

136

for myself. And, also, I've always associated with people older than I was. In school I was always a couple of years ahead of the boys my age.

Counselor: Do you know what your position in the family indicates?

(*Bronson does not; so the counselor explains briefly how the second child tends to develop a prominent ambition, and that this is accentuated when the older child is a girl.*)

Bronson: Yes, this seems to fit my case perfectly. When I was very young I can remember always trying to outdo my sister. She was rather sickly; so that made it easier. I raised such a fuss when she went to school that my parents were forced to put me in school also, though I was only four at the time. One of the reasons I studied so hard was to get ahead of my sister.

(*It is clear that Mr. Bronson is unusually objective about himself, and is able to grasp quickly the meaning of the relationships which the counselor points out. This, of course, expedites the counseling process.*)

Counselor: Can you tell me an early childhood memory? (*He briefly explains the significance of such memories.*)

Bronson: Why, yes. I guess I was about two or three when this happened. I was pushed to the fair in a little cart in which I rode backwards. While we were at the fair the pole of the cart broke and the man who worked for us had to carry me all the way home. I also remember a dream which I had many years ago. It clung so vividly to my mind that it seems like an early memory. I dreamt I was climbing up into the attic of our house on a ladder. When I got to the top rung a monkey jumped out of a green box in the attic and scared me, and I fell down the ladder. (*He laughs. The counselor by this time sees the outlines of the personality pattern, and he explains his hypothesis to the counselee.*)

Counselor: That early memory doesn't help us much, but the dream is very interesting. We can now see some rather distinct things about your personality pattern, Mr. Bronson. Let me sum them up. You work at a great tension, you said, which keeps you under a nervous strain and interferes with your creative accomplishment. We agreed that this great tension was really the expression of an exaggerated ambition, and that this ambition was connected with your inferiority feeling. Your position in the family fits into this picture. And that dream gives us some hints, too—you remember, you climbed up the ladder to the top, and then fell. Have you always been afraid of falling, or let us say, of failing?

Bronson: Why, yes, as a matter of fact I have been—very much so.

(*So far Mr. Bronson's personality pattern does not present anything particularly unique; it is the general inferiority-ambition-neurotic symptom form. Now the counselor must push the interpretation deeper to discover the unique aspects of this pattern and the consequent neurotic tendency.*)

Counselor: Why should you be afraid of failure?

Bronson: I don't know. I never have failed in any outstanding matter. But I always fear I will.

Counselor: You appear to fear some catastrophe. This usually arises out of a basic distrust of life—a feeling that one must watch carefully or some disastrous thing will happen. Do you have that feeling?

Bronson: (*thinks a moment*) Yes, I've never thought

of it in that way, but I guess I am distrustful and suspicious of life. I do have the feeling I must fight it all the time. You know, I've never been able to accept that statement of Jesus', "Be not anxious." I believe in God, but yet I have a fear and deep distrust—rather inconsistent, isn't it? (*Empathy has become very well established so that the counselor and counselee appear to be thinking along together.*)

Counselor: This distrust of life is connected with your inferiority feeling—they both represent a general feeling of insecurity. No wonder you feel you must be striving hard at all times. If you could relax that inferiority feeling, you would be able to use your creative powers more fruitfully.

Bronson: I think you're right. Now what steps shall I take to do this?

(*This is a crucial point. The counselee asks for advice. If the counselor succumbs to the temptation, with its implicit flattery, and gives advice, or even specific instructions, he short-circuits the process and thwarts the real personality readjustment of the counselee, as will be explained in the next chapter. Rather, he must seize this request for advice as a means of making the counselee accept more responsibility for himself.*)

Counselor: You wish rules on the matter. You want these rules to compel you from the outside. And you'll follow them with the same strain and tension which you manifest now. That will make your problem all the worse. Your desire for rules, you see, rises out of that same basic mistrust of life.

Bronson (*after a moment's pause*): Yes, I see that. But what am I to do?

Counselor: It is more a matter of relaxing the artificial tensions and giving your creative abilities a chance. And to do that you must understand yourself better and get over that basic distrust of life. Let's get back to the particular tension in your work which you originally described. Why do you feel you must be driven from the outside?

Bronson: Well, as you said, it is connected with my family position. I got into the habit of striving too much when I was young, and I've just been keeping it up. (*Here he attempts to explain away the problem by means of his childhood environment, and to relieve himself of responsibility by blaming a bad habit for it.*)

Counselor: No, it does not help simply to blame the habit. The habit has something to do with your present difficulty, to be sure; but it's a deeper matter than merely the changing of a habit. It is more fruitful to assume that your present exaggerated tendency to strive arises out of the same factors in your personality pattern which gave rise to your similar striving ten years ago. And what we need to understand is those factors. (*A pause. The counselee has reached a temporary impasse; the matter goes deeper than he had expected. The counselor takes a different approach, but pointing toward the same center of the problem.*) You seem to have a strong desire for perfection, Mr. Bronson, coming out of your fear of failure. Do you have a dread of being imperfect?

Bronson: Yes, I do—very strongly so. That's why I never get my articles published—I think they're not perfect.

Counselor: But you realize that nobody achieves perfection in this world? Everybody fails at some time or other.

Bronson: Yes, that's right.

Counselor: You see, if you always demand perfection, you'll never do anything. You will never take the last step on the ladder for fear you'll fail. One needs the courage of imperfection to live creatively. (*The conclusion of the interview approaches. The counselor must sum up the diagnosis and clinch it by taking advantage of the empathetic relationship between him and the counselee.*)

Counselor (*leaning forward and looking directly at the counselee*): Bronson, why do you distrust life?

Bronson: I don't know. But the more I think about it, the more I realize that I have always had this special feeling of insecurity and suspicion.

Counselor: We can understand this suspicion and distrust of life as coming out of your inferiority feeling, which was accentuated by your small size in your youth, and your family position. But you are no longer inferior—you occupy a good position and certainly enjoy more security than most people in the world. So you do not need to fight life so desperately now. You can afford to *trust* more. All these fears and staying awake nights and the great strains are unnecessary. You can get along better without them. That exaggerated fear of failure is a bogey; you are not in danger of failing. The dream may have been true once, but it is not now; and you don't need to be worried for fear a monkey will jump out and scare you. So you can take on courage and let this unnecessary inferiority feeling evaporate. You can develop the courage of imperfection, and in that way you'll relax much of that driving ambition. You need to give your creative abilities a chance. That means trusting and affirming life more. And it means affirming yourself, so that you will be able to create without being forced from the outside.

(*Counselor and counselee have been looking directly at each other. The latter reflects for a moment as he becomes aware of the new possibilities before him. As he gets up to go, Bronson expresses his gratitude to the counselor, and says, as he stands at the door:*)

Bronson: Say, I think that distrust of life explains why I have become so interested lately in supernatural theology. By this I was able to look down on the world, and condemn man and conclude that the world was all bad and nothing could be expected but catastrophe. I now see that this attitude is probably connected with my general pessimism about life.

Counselor: Possibly it is; you know more about that than I. You might turn these questions over in your mind in the future, Mr. Bronson—the questions of your basic distrust of life and why you feel you must be compelled from the outside. You'll continually get new insights into how your difficulties arise out of your personality pattern, and thus you'll become increasingly better able to understand yourself.

\* \* \*

Before we discuss the confession stage in general, let us make clear again that the above is not to be regarded as a typical case by which other interviews are to be judged. For Mr. Bronson possessed much more ability to look at himself objectively than most counselees, and therefore the interview moved much more rapidly than we should ordinarily expect. Whereas this interview lasted two hours, it would customarily require three or maybe four hour periods to penetrate as deeply into the personality pattern. Then, too, the factors in Mr. Bronson's personality fitted together unusually clearly. The counselor should be ready to expect ordinarily a more difficult task in discovering the basic relationships within the personality.

Let us note, also, that this case did not end with a cure. Its purpose was to illustrate confession and interpretation; and the matter of the cure, i.e. transformation, will be discussed in the next chapter. What we wished to do was to enlighten Mr. Bronson, to help him understand himself;

and it was not at all expected that his personality would be re-made when he stepped out the door. There was a process of transformation set in motion, of course, on the basis of *understanding* and *suggestion*, which are curative forces that we shall discuss below. But this interview did not vanquish Mr. Bronson's difficulty—it fitted him, rather, to vanquish it for himself. What such an interview accomplishes is to be observed after a couple of months, when the suggestions have had time to work themselves out in the counselee's daily living. But all this is the province of the next chapter.

Some important guides for the counselor arising from our general discussion of confession are, first, the principle that *the counselee does the talking* in the confession period. This point, of course, is obvious; but it must be stressed, for unless the counselee "talks it out" with some degree of thoroughness the counseling will not get to the root of the matter. It can almost be made a rule: if the counselee does not do at least two-thirds of the talking in a given hour, something is wrong with the counseling procedure. The counselor should be chary about his own talking; every word he utters should have a purpose.

It is well for us to realize, as the second guide, that there is a *cathartic value in confession per se*. The mere fact that the counselee has talked his problem out, in the presence of an objective and understanding counselor, has made him psychologically healthier. It has relieved him of some of his inhibitions; it has made possible a more ready flow from his subconscious to his conscious by flushing the channel; and it has helped him see his problems in the clarifying light of objectivity. This does not mean that confession to any person who happens to be at hand will bring the same reward, be it the cook in the fraternity house or a shepherd on the hillside. The function of empathy is such that the person to whom one is confessing has much to do with the cathartic value of the confession.

The skilful counselor, thirdly, is able to *turn the counselee's confession to the central problem.* Unlike Mr. Bronson, most counselees will tend to procrastinate and ramble about among minor topics, putting off the fated moment when they must confess the real problem. There are certain unconscious processes in the individual, as a matter of fact, which make him involuntarily shy away from the delicate area of his difficulty. This means that skill is required on the part of the counselor to perceive the real problem underneath the irrelevant statements. The common practice of letting the counselee begin anywhere in his talking is sound, but the counselor then must open the way for him to talk about the real problem.

For the period of the confession, the counselor must be *incapable of being shocked or offended.* There was nothing in the above case to offend; but in most cases, if one goes deeply enough, there comes to light material the mere hearing of which would shock many persons. But if the counselor is shocked or offended, he forfeits his right at that moment to be a counselor—for such a reaction is a sign that his own ego has insinuated itself into the picture. Being offended is, in fact, a way of withdrawing and protecting one's self. He who is shocked by the use of certain sex words, or the description of certain sex practices, cannot qualify as a counselor in these areas. This is particularly important because many counselees will attempt, consciously or unconsciously, to shock the listener. That is one expression of their neurosis. And if the listener is shocked, the counselee's neurosis becomes all the worse, and the value of the present interview is destroyed. Calm objectivity, which is based on the realization that nothing which is human is foreign or unworthy of understanding, is the attitude for the counselor.

*Emotional upsets* must not be permitted during the confession period. To have the counselee crying on one's shoulder is a sign, not so much of the success of the counselor as confidant, but of the mismanagement of the interview. There is a tendency for counselees to become emotionally upset, for they are expressing ideas and fears and suppressed material which they have possibly never told to anyone else. Many of them break down and cry. Here is where the counselor must exercise his skill by remaining calm and making sure this calm carries, by means of empathy, into the counselee. Sometimes it may be advisable to let the counselee cry a little, but as soon as the tension has been released the counselor will bring him back again to emotional equilibrium. This is why the counselor should be chary about giving out sympathy in the interview; for sympathy, when it is personal and subjective, can augment the emotional upsets. Empathy is the better attitude because it is objective and includes all that is valuable of sympathy. Its importance cannot be overestimated, for in empathy lies the secret of controlling the mood of the interview.

Turning now to the interpretation stage of the interview, we find several important guides for counselors. First, *interpretation is a function of the counselor and counselee working together*. It is not at all a case of the counselor's figuring out the pattern and then presenting it on a platter to the other.

And this brings us to the more specific point, the counselor *suggests interpretations* rather than stating them dogmatically. He does not say, "This is this," but rather, "This *appears* to be this," or, "This is *connected* with this"; and in each case he waits to see how the counselee reacts to the suggestion. For as we have stated previously, all conclusions in personality matters are of the nature of hypotheses; and the truth of the hypothesis is contingent upon the way it works in the personality at hand.

This leads to a third observation; the counselor must be able *to read the meaning of the counselee's reactions to suggestions.* If the counselee accepts the counselor's suggested interpretation, as Mr. Bronson so often did, by saying calmly, "Yes, I think that is true," the suggestion may be accepted by both for the time being. But if the counselee is quite indifferent, the suggestion not seeming to make any difference, the counselor discards the idea, concluding he has not yet struck anything very significant. If, in the third place, the counselee rejects the suggestion violently, protesting vehemently that it is untrue, the counselor may tentatively conclude that the suggestion *is* probably the correct interpretation and that he has struck close to the root of the problem. But he must never insist at the time. He merely retreats, takes another lead, and from this new angle approaches the same center of the problem. If he is successful in hitting upon the true interpretation, he will suddenly find his counselee giving up his resistance and admitting the truth even of the originally rejected suggestion.

We shall conclude this section with a word on the limitations of the counselor's technique. He cannot expect to uncover the total personality pattern of the individual; it is not, in fact, his province to do so. His function, rather, is first to listen objectively and thus help the counselee confess and "air" all aspects of the problem; second, to aid the counselee to understand the deeper sources in his personality from which the problem arises; and third, to point out relationships which will give the counselee a new understanding of himself and equip him thereby to solve the problem for himself. The less experienced the counselor is, the more should his function be confined to the confession stage, with interpretation suggested only tentatively. But as he becomes more experienced he is increasingly able to offer fruitful interpretations which will help disclose the deeper relationships in the personality pattern.

## USE OF TESTS, RECORDS, ETC.

TESTS and questionnaires and other standardized forms for obtaining basic information about personalities can be useful if employed with discretion. If the counselor is in a college situation, he can often obtain suitable forms, such as vocational aptitude tests and personal prejudice tests, from the psychology or sociology departments of the institution. Oftentimes the college authorities are willing to co-operate to the extent of making available to the counselor the intelligence quotient of the student as shown in the entrance examination. The counselor will probably find himself working out his own questionnaire for obtaining personality information. This should include the basic items we have suggested previously, such as family and background, age, matters like physical health, hobbies, special interests, and friendships.

But the caution in regard to the use of tests is obvious: all data obtained therefrom is to be regarded as secondary and supplementary to the personal interview. The particular merit of tests, it appears, is in group work, not individual. And although they can be employed with individuals, if for no other reason than the convenience of the standardized record for handling and keeping basic information, their results are always to be regarded as corroborative and never definitive in themselves. The person is the end; and whenever forms and records obscure the infinite variety and unpredictability of the individual, they should be discarded.

It is advisable for the counselor to keep some notation of the various facts in the case, if only for the purpose of forcing himself to be objective and of restraining his wishful thinking. My practice has been to jot down the essential facts while the counselee is talking in the confession stage, always however, requesting his permission beforehand and assuring him the notes will be destroyed if he desires at the conclusion of the counseling series. This notation gives a professional and business-like touch to the interview. It is a way of keeping all aspects of the picture before one. Still another value is that the counselor is then afforded an opportunity to study the facts between consultations and possibly gain some new insights into the counselee's personality pattern. After casual moments of counseling, such as on hikes or chance walks in the evening, I often jot down the significant facts about the individual as background for my future contacts with him.

How many periods of consultation should the counselor plan to hold in a given case? This varies, of course. Many times one consultation is all that is practicable. But in every case where it is desired to penetrate somewhat deeply into the personality pattern, in instances, for example, of distinct personality difficulties, it is advisable to plan arbitrarily for a series of interviews. The plan I customarily follow consists of six interviews lasting one hour each, spaced at two a week. An appointment is made for a definite hour, rather than leaving it simply as a matter of "dropping in next week." This period of three weeks gives both parties—particularly the counselee—time to reflect on the insights discovered in each successive interview; and by reason of the assimilative and selective processes of the unconsciousness, the counseling takes up at a deeper level each time.

Long periods of consultation are not to be recommended. Occasionally student directors tell of three and four hour interviews of an evening; but such affairs are usually connected with emotional strain, which befuddles the counseling. After a certain period both counselor and counselee lose the power to be objective, and subjective attitudes are bound to creep in. Ordinarily, we may conclude, one hour is the optimum duration for an interview.

*Chapter VII*

## THE TRANSFORMING OF PERSONALITY

WE NOW CONSIDER the final stage in the counseling procedure, the consummation and goal of the whole process—the transforming of the counselee's personality. In the confession and interpretation stages we found that the source of his problem was a faulty adjustment of tensions within his personality. This maladjustment, it was observed, went hand in hand with his mistaken attitudes toward life. The wrong attitudes must be corrected and thus a readjustment of the tensions effected. This is called "transforming" because it does give the personality a new "form"; it changes, not necessarily the content, but certainly the structure; it is a readjustment of the constellation of tensions which constitutes the form of the personality.

In the counseling process we do not remold the person completely and send him out of the office a new man. The endeavor is to free him to be himself. This means giving him the start in his own task of transforming his personality.

And how is this to be done?

In the first place, *personality is not transformed by advice.* This misconception we must destroy once and for all; true counseling and the giving of advice are distinctly different functions. Sometimes, of course, everyone is put in the role of adviser: the dean must advise the freshman about certain courses of which he as yet knows nothing, or one must advise the stranger which streetcar to take down town. But in neither of these cases is the personality of the individual being dealt with. No deep understanding, and very little empathy, enters into the process. Advice (using the term in its everyday sense) is always superficial; it is a handing down of directions from above, a one-way traffic. True counseling operates in a much deeper sphere, and its conclusions are always the product of two personalities working together on the same level.

The psychotherapists do not mince words in their rejection of the position of adviser. Many quotations could be cited of the same tenor as the following one from Freud: "Moreover, I assure you that you are misinformed if you assume that advice and guidance in the affairs of life is an integral part of the analytic influence. On the contrary, we reject this role of the mentor as far as possible. Above all, we wish to attain independent decisions on the part of the patient." [1]

Advice-giving is not an adequate counseling function because it violates the autonomy of personality. It has been agreed that personality must be free and autonomous; how, then, can one person justifiably pass ready-made decisions down to another? Ethically one cannot do it; and practically one cannot—for advice from above can never effect any real change in the other's personality. The idea never becomes part of him, and he will cast it off at the earliest convenience. Practically speaking, however, the counselor is often called on to give advice in matters that are not strictly personality problems. Here he may do so from time to time, but let it be clear in his mind that he is not genuinely counseling at that moment.

Sometimes advice may work legitimately as suggestion, the individual thus remaking the decision for himself. But this represents a different process, which we shall consider below. The important consideration is that every decision of account must come, in the end, from the counselee himself. "In my view," Rank aptly says, "the patient should make himself what he is, should will it and do it himself, without force or justification and without need to shift the responsibility for it." [2]

Turning now to the positive means of transforming personality, let us first consider the *leaven of suggestion*. Suggestion is often condemned as a technique in personality influence, but that is due to a misconception; rightly understood, suggestion is seen to play an inescapable role in all personal development. Every individual is continually receiving suggestions of every sort from his environment. The pertinent question is, why does he accept certain suggestions and reject others? The answer lies in the nature of his personality pattern. It is not accurate to attribute the downfall of an individual to the suggestion of someone in his environment, or to some book he read, or to anything else external. We must ask, as was suggested in an earlier chapter, what was there in this individual's personality pattern which would permit him to accept the suggestions from outside?

Every individual has tendencies toward many different forms of behavior. We can think of each person's unconscious as throbbing with a number of instinctive "pushes" knocking for expression in the outside world. To use Plato's time-honored figure, there are in the unconscious a number of horses straining at the bit to be off in different directions. In the healthy individual the conscious ego selects from this variety the direction of which it approves, and restrains the other tendencies. Neurosis means a weakening of the ego's guidance, an inability to decide in which direction the movement should be made, and hence a crippling of effective action. Now a suggestion from the environment may be the touch needed to loose one of these tendencies which is already strong within the individual.

The counselor cannot escape using suggestion in some form, so he may as well be intelligent about his use of it. During counseling he may throw out a number of suggestions as a fisherman does certain kinds of flies, waiting to see which fly the trout will leap to catch. Many of the suggestions will appear to have no effect; but others will suddenly be seized by the counselee, will be accepted into his mind and there loosed to work like a leaven. The suggestion of the counselor here becomes coupled with a tendency already in the unconscious, and the combination may be enough to bring the counselee to a decision. In this case the counselee has been enabled to draw into expression some new phase of his unconscious, and he moves forward with his self more unified.

In some cases, therefore, the most useful function of the counselor is *to lay all the constructive alternatives before the counselee.* From these alternatives his unconscious selective process will choose what it needs.

It is the purpose of a book like this, for example, to throw out numerous suggestions in somewhat organized form on the subject of counseling, not with the hope—heaven forbid!—that anyone use the book like a mathematics table, but rather with the expectation that the suggestions will combine creatively with the tendencies already in the reader's mind and thus give birth to an understanding of counseling that will be uniquely the brainchild of the reader.

The second factor in the transforming of personality

is the *creative function of understanding*. This is to say, brusquely, that in the very understanding of the problem some transformation in the personality of the counselee takes place. It is the basic assumption of Adlerian therapy that if the patient understands truly he will act rightly, the modern development of the old Socratic maxim "Knowing is doing." Certainly there is basic truth in this contention that knowledge leads to virtue; it is an assumption which is made to some degree by all psychotherapy. Knowing the truth does imply some compulsion to do the truth; for if it be really true, one's happiness and future welfare depend upon doing it. It has been pointed out above that neurotic forms of behavior are forms of self-deceit, and that if this deceit be unmasked—i.e., the rationalization and false motives removed—the ego will be forced to relax its self-defeating training-formulae and direct itself into socially constructive forms of behavior.

In the stage of interpretation the counselor automatically employs this method of transforming character, for he endeavors to give the counselee understanding of the factors which have led him into his difficulties. In this very understanding a creative activity will automatically be set in motion in the counselee's mind to correct the mistakes.

We observed in the previous chapter how the creative function of understanding worked in the case of Mr. Bronson. As an epitomizing of the interpretation, the counselor suggested two specific questions to Mr. Bronson with the intention that these questions should work like searchlights in Bronson's mind in the future, continually pointing out to him new insights into his personality problem and thus aiding him toward clarification. Surely enough, Mr. Bronson returned a few days later to tell how he had suddenly awakened out of a phantasy as he was

154

riding on the subway and discovered that he had been subconsciously pondering and worrying for fifteen minutes
about how he was to find time to prepare his lectures.
"This fits in with the attitude of insecurity which we found
in my personality," he said. And in this instance he had
simply laughed at how his old pattern was endeavoring to
work him into a useless nervous tension as it had customarily done in the past—and his laughing served temporarily
to relieve the tension. Thus as this understanding more
and more works in Mr. Bronson's mind, consciously, but
even more unconsciously, he will move in geometric progression toward personality health.

But knowledge is not the whole of virtue, and understanding is not all one needs to transform personality. And
so it is necessary to move on to further considerations.

The third means of transforming character is one implied in an earlier chapter, *the influence resulting from the
empathetic relationship.* The two personalities being to an
extent merged, influence must inevitably flow from the
counselor to the counselee. This means that the counselor
can affect some transformation of the other's character
merely by directing his own mood and his own willing
during the empathetic relationship.

Rank points out that his method in therapy is to make
it possible for the patient to identify himself with the
therapist's positive will, the patient thus taking on extra
strength to triumph over his own negative will. Thereupon the patient learns to will positively and constructively. I assume this is very much the same process that we
have been explaining in terms of empathy.

In counseling I make it a specific practice near the
end of the interview to *will courage*, knowing that this
courage will carry over into the will of the counselee.
During the *confession* we have both become pessimistic,

for his despair has carried into my mood; then in the *interpretation* we have progressed toward a clarified view of the situation; and as the solution to the problem and the new mode of behavior present themselves, courage has taken the place of the despair. I know that my courage, as counselor, will become his whether I make specific statements of courage or not, for our psychic states are to an extent identified. This willing courage may sound like sending the counselee out with a "psychological boost"; but if it is that, it is a "boost" which is a relatively deep function in personality.

To give a simple illustration. A student at a formal tea is standing in the corner, shy and embarrassed and in general having a poor time. As counselor you walk over with the intention of helping him out of his negative mood. Suppose you try the method of advice; you clap him on the shoulder and say enthusiastically, "Buck up, old man, smile and have a good time." He then makes a feeble attempt to buck up, puts on a forced smile, feels all the more guilty about his shyness, and so gets even more embarrassed. His second state is worse than the first. Or suppose you try the method of suggestion; you remark, "A lot of interesting people here. This is a good chance to get to know them." Now he has already thought that—at least thought that he should be thinking it—and so the suggestion may do some good. But the best method is the empathetic one. You first allow your psychic states to become merged by taking on his mood, and you may remark something to this effect, "Too bad these teas have to be so formal. It's pretty hard to feel at home." The shy boy brightens up and answers with genuine enthusiasm, "Yes, it certainly is!" for this is exactly the idea that has been uppermost in his mind. Empathy is achieved, but in achieving it you have surrendered some of your own happiness to take on his unhappiness. But after a moment's conversation you again perceive the possibilities in the tea, and your optimism and courage return. This time he takes on your mood, which overcomes his shyness and embarrassment. And the conclusion of our parable would be that he begins to move about the room with courage and interest in the other people.

The fourth factor in the transforming of character is the *utilization of suffering*. The counselor may channel the suffering of the neurotic counselee to furnish the power to bring about the transformation of character.

A human being will not change his personality pattern, when all is said and done, until he is forced to do so by his own suffering. Advice, persuasion, requests from the outside will effect only a temporary change in the cloak of the personality. And here is where mere rational understanding is shown to be inadequate, for it takes a dynamic stronger than simply an abstract idea that another way would be "better" to bring about a real change. The human ego is a recalcitrant and stubborn affair; it fights off disturbance, for it very much fears the profound insecurity that comes when its style of life is shaken. In fact, many neurotic individuals prefer to endure the misery of their present situation than to risk the uncertainty that would come with change. No matter how clearly the neurosis may be shown to be based on sheer falsehood, the patient will not give it up until his suffering becomes insupportable.

Fortunately the wheels of life do grind relentlessly on and bring a just portion of suffering as a penalty for every neurotic attitude. When this misery becomes so great that the individual is willing to give up his wrong attitude, in fact to give up everything, he has arrived at that state of desperation which Kunkel says is prerequisite for any cure at all. We can agree that this state of desperation is required; but since in counseling we deal ordinarily with minor cases of personality difficulty, the desperation may be limited to the area of the particular problem.

Fortunately every wrong attitude brings its suffering, but unfortunately most persons do not use this suffering constructively. The neurotic will turn this suffering back into a vicious circle. For example, the counselee, say a shy student, suffers from painful embarrassment at a college social function, and therefore resolves not to go to any more parties. This of course makes his problem all the worse. It is the function of the counselor to channel this suffering constructively, i.e., to connect it with the mistaken attitude. This will mean pointing out to the student that his suffering is really due to his egocentricity, his lack of social interest, at the party, and that staying away will be an expression of even greater egocentricity and therefore will make his suffering ultimately all the worse.

Suffering is one of the most potentially creative forces in nature. It is not sentimentality to relate the greatness of certain characters to their sufferings. As the pearl is produced in the endeavor of the clam to adjust itself to the irritation of the grain of sand, so the great works of Poe and Shelley and Van Gogh and Dostoevski are understandable only in relation to the sufferings these artists experienced.

Jung expresses this truth: "But all creativeness in the realm of the spirit as well as every psychic advance of man arises from a state of mental suffering." [3] And Kunkel, who has most profoundly explored the meaning of suffering in personality development, points out that the vicious circle of suffering may become constructive. "When we see that the pain is the first step toward being reborn, and that all that has happened, no matter how miserable, is only a necessary step toward clarification, no sorrow or torment, or even joy has been in vain." [4]

People should then rejoice in suffering, strange as it sounds, for this is the sign of the availability of energy to transform their characters. Suffering is nature's method of indicating a mistaken attitude or way of behavior, and to the objective and non-egocentric person every moment of suffering is the opportunity for growth. In this sense we can be "glad we're neurotic"—glad, that is, if we are able to utilize the suffering.

A counseling principle arises here: *the counselor should not relieve his counselee of suffering, but rather redirect the suffering into constructive channels.* He should use this suffering like water power which, when rightly channeled, generates the dynamic capable of effecting the personality transformation.

The counselor should not assume any of the individual's final responsibility for working out his own salvation. In severe cases he may assume some of the responsibility temporarily, but only to give it back in more definite form to the counselee in the end. This principle is the basis for the practice of guarding against any intimate social relationships with the counselee during the period—assuming this lasts for several weeks—of the counseling. In these social contacts the counselee will be almost certain to involve the counselor in his web of responsibility, assuming unconsciously, for example, that the counselor likes him so well he will not let him fail. And thus he shifts some of the responsibility to the other's shoulders. Calm objectivity, rather, is the best attitude during the duration of the counseling period.

It is sometimes said that the counselee should always go out of the office happier than he entered. But this may indicate that the counseling was merely a reassuring of his old style of life. The patting on the back may do him definite harm and postpone the final overcoming of the difficulty. He should ordinarily go out more *courageous* after the interview, but courageous with the painful realization that he must transform his personality. If the counseling has been more than superficial, he will feel shaken and will probably be unhappy in his present situation.

At the conclusion of the interview the counselee may feel some deep anger (which he may not even be conscious of at the time) toward the counselor, this man who has pointed out to him uncomfortable truths which he has been struggling for years to keep hidden. But this anger will soon be redirected to his own mistaken personality pattern, and he will then be profoundly grateful for the counselor's help. This case is probably typical: in a conference recently the counselee and I unearthed some truths which she found very disagreeable. Consequently she exhibited a negative attitude toward me for several days after the interview. I noticed this, of course, and interpreted it as a possible indication that we had hit upon her basic problem. Surely enough, a half week later she came to me with apologies for her negative attitude (which, however, she assumed I had not observed!) and explained that she had accepted our diagnosis and was frankly facing the need to transform her personality.

Cases are often met in which the dynamic initiative to give up the neurotic pattern is absent. In the interpretation stage the counselee may abstractly see the value of transforming his character, but he says to himself, "Not yet." Then the counselor in most cases can only wait, knowing that when life in its own good time has piled upon this individual the suffering his egocentricity merits, he will bring himself humbly to make the change. Suffering in this case would be a boon.

On rare occasions the skilled counselor can bring the suffering of the other person to a head in anticipation of the crisis. Recently an individual with whose style of life I had become very familiar wrote me that he had grown completely discouraged, that he felt life was unfair to him, and that he contemplated dropping out of school and bumming west. And at the conclusion of the outburst he asked my counsel. In the answering letter I aimed specifically to bring his suffering to a head. I pointed out that his attitude was that of a pampered child and that his unhappiness was due to his self-pity and lack of courage to manage in his situation. I intentionally left no loophole in the letter for his ego-prestige. For several weeks I did not hear from him, but when the answer did come it was full of gratitude and assurances that my diagnosis had been correct and that he had already progressed far in overcoming the wrong attitudes.

This is not to be described as giving the individual a "jolt," or bringing him suffering he would otherwise have escaped. It is rather the drawing to a head of suffering that was potentially present, and thus averting a worse crisis. Needless to say, the counselor will not utilize this rather delicate method until he has become quite skilled.

The counselor's function, to summarize, is to connect the individual's suffering with the neurotic aspects of his personality pattern. Dealing with an individual over a period of time, the counselor can point out each week the way the sufferings of the individual during the past week were related to his mistaken attitudes and behavior. He can even predict suffering, pointing out to the counselee that the next time he suffers from embarrassment at a social function or from quarreling with his family, it will be due to such and such a factor in his personality. Thus the grinding of nature's relentless wheels will be made to serve for good.

Finally, after all our discussion, we come to the realization that there is a great area in the transformation of personality which we do not understand, and which we can attribute only to *the mysterious creativity of life*. This lad has come in with a hang-dog expression, timid, shy, feeling inferior at every turn—he appears defeated in the game of life before getting well started. But somehow the chrysalis of his narrow self-concern is broken; he is transferred to the objective, expansive, and constructive side of life. His despair has given birth to hope, his selfishness has been replaced by unselfishness, his cowardice has changed to courage, his pain is outshone by joy, and his loneliness is being vanquished by love. In this transformation of personality we, as counselors, may have had some small thing to do. But we know we have not remade the person. We know we have done precious little —merely guided a bit here, directed a bit there; and the creative forces of life have effected the miracle of transformation.

As the motto has it, "The physician furnishes the conditions—God works the cure." [5] Like the doctor, we may bind up the wound; but there are all the forces of life welling up in their incalculable spontaneity in the growing together of skin and nerve tissues and the reflowing of blood to perform the healing. Before the creative forces of life, the true counselor stands humbly. And his humility is not of the false sort, for the deeper his understanding of personality the more clearly he realizes how minute his efforts in comparison to the greatness of the whole. He says with the psalmist, "Lord, this is too wonderful for me." I am myself frank to say that when the limits of my own understanding are reached, I understand the miracle of the transformation of personality in terms of that age-old but ever-new concept, the grace of God.

# PART THREE
## ULTIMATE CONSIDERATIONS

"It's here [a lunatic asylum] that men are most themselves—themselves and nothing but themselves—sailing with outspread sails of self. Each shuts himself in a cask of self, the cask stopped with a bung of self and seasoned in a well of self. None has a tear for others' woes or cares what any other thinks. . . . .

"Now surely you'll say that he's himself! He's full of himself and nothing else; himself in every word he says—himself when he's beside himself. . . . .

"Long live the Emperor of Self!"
HENRIK IBSEN, *Peer Gynt,*
ACT IV, SCENE 13.

"Whosoever shall seek to gain his life shall lose it: but whosoever shall lose his life shall preserve it."
LUKE 17: 33

*Chapter VIII*

# THE PERSONALITY OF THE COUNSELOR

## WHAT MAKES A GOOD COUNSELOR

THE PERSONAL EQUATION is all-important in counseling—the counselor can work only through himself, and it is therefore essential that this self be an effective instrument. All the therapists, and certainly the previous arguments of this book, would support Adler's statement, "The technique of treatment must be in yourself."

The superficial qualities of the good counselor are self-evident: winsomeness, general physical attractiveness, the ability to be at ease in other people's company, and other characteristics which are equally ambiguous in meaning. These qualities are not innate but acquired; one is not a "born" counselor but a developed one. And the development comes as a consequence of the counselor's own clarification and his interest and enjoyment of other people. To put it bluntly, if the counselor genuinely—that is, *objectively*—enjoys the company of others and wishes their interest, he finds himself automatically being the kind of person that attracts them. So often we find that the person who is not liked is he who in his unconscious does not want to be liked, either because of the requirements other people's affections would make of him or because of the wish for solitariness. "Personal attractiveness" is a term often used but exasperatingly seldom defined; we can define it as the reverse side of one's own interest and enjoyment of people.

But to penetrate more deeply into the problem, what differentiates a good counselor from a poor one? Is it training? Some training would appear necessary, but it is easy to see that prolonged graduate work in experimental psychology as it is at present taught would not necessarily fit one for effective counseling—and might even unfit one. Freud expresses our answer classically when, in pointing out that medical training is not necessary as a prerequisite for the psychoanalyst, he states that the quality which is essential is "inherent insight into the human soul—first of all into the unconscious layers of his own soul—and *practical training*." [1]

Insight "first of all into the unconscious layers of his own soul." That is the key. This means the ability to escape from one's ego-bias, to escape the tendency to counsel on the basis of one's own prejudices. This ego-bias is so stubborn a hydra-headed monster that one must exercise all one's ingenuity in overcoming it. The case of a student, for example, who had shifted around among many professional schools and finally ended up in a theological seminary, was presented to a seminar I recently held with a group of persons in religious vocations. There was the immediate consensus in the group that, though the young man had vacillated unfortunately, he had at last found his right niche! If the group had been one of doctors, and the student had at last found his way into a medical school, the approval would have been as evident. Seeing others through one's own prejudices—this ego-bias is clearly the worst stumbling block in the personality of the counselor.

How is the ego-bias to be removed? It cannot be eradicated entirely, but it can be understood and guarded against. For this reason the various schools of psychotherapy insist that the applicant for their field must first be thoroughly analyzed himself in order to understand and remove as many as possible of his own complexes. If he were not, it is certain he would not be able to avoid treating patients in terms of these complexes.

It would unquestionably be wise for the counselor to be analyzed by a psychotherapist. This discussion of his own personality with another would give him a priceless understanding of himself and hence aid him tremendously in effectively counseling others. It does not mean that he would be taken apart piece by piece by the psychotherapist; his is not a psychotic case; treatment would be a matter of the therapist's assisting him to understand himself. The right choice of a therapist is of course important. We can predict that this constructive form of psychological analysis will be considered a requisite part of the training of teachers, ministers, and social workers in future generations.

But most would-be counselors will not be in a position for sustained consultations with a psychotherapist. The next best way, as the Freudian Forsyte puts it, is to analyze one's self. It will not be possible to do this completely—the ego is too clever to be tracked down in its inmost lair without outside assistance—but one can go a long way toward understanding one's self, and this will suit the immediate needs of most counselors. It is my hope that this book, together with other books in the field, will help the reader to a psychological understanding of himself. When the counselor has conscientiously gone as far as he can in analyzing himself, it is helpful to have even one or two sittings with a psychotherapist or another counselor to help him see the particular quirks by which his ego deceives itself.

## ANALYSIS OF A TYPICAL RELIGIOUS COUNSELOR

To HELP the reader in his task of understanding himself, I shall present here an analysis of religious counselors in general. This is a boiling down of the characteristics I have found recurring in a number of persons in the religious vocation who have consulted with me, and it should result in some sort of picture of the "typical neurosis" of people in this field. After presenting this picture at a recent conference of religious workers, I was accosted by several persons in the group with an insistent, "That was I," or, "You were really talking about me, weren't you?" Of course I had the pleasure of assuring them that it was no one in particular, and that if the shoe fitted them, I must have succeeded in my task of catching the typical neurotic characteristics toward which religious workers tend. It is my hope that many readers will see themselves in the following analysis to a great enough extent to derive real help in understanding their own patterns.

What characteristics do we observe in the typical religious worker? First, that he works hard and conscientiously. He appears not to relax as often as people in other vocations, and does not have as many avocational interests. He is apt to throw himself entirely into his job, even taking conscious pride in this fact. He works at a tension, and in fact tends to carry this tension through twenty-four hours of the day, for his job is such as not to be limited by working hours. Sometimes this tension becomes so great that he finds it difficult to take vacations or holidays without a guilty feeling.

This typical religious worker carries responsibility well. He is careful about details in social as well as vocational matters—in fact so careful of details as sometimes to irritate people around him. We observe in him a great desire not to fail. The dread of failure, though normal when connected with important matters, is here exaggerated and connected with minor and unimportant things.

All of these observations point to the fact that the religious worker follows what Rank calls the "all or none" law, throwing himself headlong into whatever he does with a lack of ability to respond partially to situations. This lack of ability to partialize is connected with his lack of interests and friends outside his work, the failure to enjoy the means of life, and a preoccupation with absolute ends. One of the chief characteristics of the neurotic individual, incidentally, is a tendency toward complete concern with ends, which become absolute and rigid in his mind.

Where there is great tension, a fear of failure in small things, and an unsually great concern for details, we suspect that strong ambition is present also. Surely enough, the typical religious worker does possess an exaggerated ambition. He is particularly convinced of the indispensability and importance of his work, and we see him hurrying about here and there as though the world depended on it.

Please do not misunderstand: a normal conviction of the importance of one's work is healthy and desirable. But when it is expressed in a lasting tension in the worker, we can conclude that his ego-pattern has become too much involved in the job. It is *his* vocation; and because he has an exaggerated feeling of his own importance, his job must automatically be the world's most important. That is why people remark about such individuals, "He takes himself too seriously." The judgment, "He takes his work too seriously," may express almost the same over-evaluation of one's self. A certain form of ambition is healthy and normal—the non-egocentric form, which is a spontaneous expression of the individual's creative abili-

169

ties. This form permits one occasional periods of relaxation. But when the individual works with never relaxing tension, we become suspicious that the motive is his ego-striving rather than the unselfish desire to contribute to humanity.

We might call this exaggerated ambition, as it shows itself in so-called religious people, the "Messiah complex." It is the person's conviction of the indispensability of his own person, and the consequent feeling that his particular work is indispensable to humanity and the universe. Thus he is given a mask for his pride, and sets himself up as a reformer, moral judge over his fellows, and proceeds to speak *ex cathedra*. It may be one's belief that there is no more important work in the world than that of religion, but that does not mean that it could not go on without one. This work is devoted to the glory of God, not of the egoistic individual; and we have a right to expect a humility, a sense of the minuteness of man's efforts compared to the greatness and power of God. The religious worker serves Christ; he is not Christ.

One has only to glance through history to see how dangerous this "Messiah complex" can become. How many a terrible inquisition was given demonic power by the fact that its progenitors persuaded themselves they were doing Christ's will! This becomes an excuse for the waiving of the last vestiges of conscience and humane feeling; and the self-styled "holy man" who is merely using his holy vocation as a cloak for his own ego-striving is more demonic (witness the crusaders in Constantinople) than the purely secular man. It is needless to add that the fact that this ego-motive behind the "Messiah complex" is unconscious only makes the point the truer. In the typical religious worker the process is unconscious, and it requires an objective point of view to determine how unselfish is the motivation behind the zeal. The prestige of God used as the camouflage for one's own desire for domination—how ironically tragic that religion can be so misused! [2]

It is also observable that the typical religious worker has not solved the problem of his sexual adjustment with particular success. Some persons in religious vocations appear not to feel the normal attraction for members of the opposite sex; but this apparent quiescence of the sexual urges may be evidence of a misdirection which may result in the impulses springing out later in more troublesome form. The tendency to rule out the sex function itself, as exhibited in the endeavor to think of marriage chiefly in terms of having a home and children, often indicates that the sex problem has not been honestly confronted.[3]

We can understand this failure to meet the sex problem as a product of our culture, which contains unfortunate strains of condemnation of the sex act itself and consequent tendencies to separate it from normal life. These influences come down with particular force upon individuals in religious vocations. Oftentimes religious and social workers use the concept of "sublimation" as a rationalization of their failure to make an adequate attempt to solve their sex problem. But sublimation, curious Freudian term that it is, does not have the meaning popularly given it in religious circles. Freud was endeavoring when he employed this term to explain social and artistic activities as one aspect of libido expression; he certainly did not mean that one can plunge into art or social service and thereby be totally relieved of his sexual impulses. It is possible, of course, for the individual to reduce the tension in his whole organism by work and exercise and enthusiastic participation in the not specifically sexual aspects of social activity—and to this limited extent the popular meaning given the term sublimation is accurate. But one still has the normal sexual urge, and he may well come to grips with the necessity of sexual deprivation if that is the situation.

Of course it is possible to live well without specific sexual expression, but the means of doing so is honest and frank facing of the situation, not dishonest repression. The endeavor to ignore and cover up the sex factor is in most cases clear dishonesty, and actually amounts to a "submerging" of the urge, in Dr. Oliver Butterfield's phrase, rather than sublimation. Many people do find themselves in positions where sexual deprivation is the situation; the courageous and psychologically healthy adjustment in that case is to admit the deprivation and frankly make the renunciation that is necessary. Even married persons must still face this aspect of their lives with some ability for renunciation in certain situations. And the unmarried person who faces his problem honestly, escaping neither into repression or libertinism, but exercising the courage to bear the necessary tensions, will be in the best position eventually to solve his love and marriage problem satisfactorily.

What are the results of the failure to solve the sex problem in the work of the religious counselor? First, he or she is clearly unfitted to advise others in the area of sex. The counselor must be on guard against forcing his own maladjustments upon others, and if his own sex problem is inadequately handled he must step very cautiously in that area in his counseling.

In the second place, the religious worker with an unsolved sex problem may make emotional attachments which are harmful to the persons with whom he or she works. Particularly is this true if the individual is specifically trying to "sublimate" in these other persons. We could cite the actual case of a women's student worker who thinks of the students part of the time as her children (this is conscious) and part of the time as her sweethearts (this, of course, is unconscious but evident to any intelligent observer). This introduces a subjective element which makes effective counseling impossible. One of the counselor's hardest tasks is to keep the counselee from becoming attached to him or her; and if the readiness for emotional attachment is present on the counselor's side too, the counseling relationship is irreparably ruined. Whenever the counselor finds himself taking subjective pleasure in the presence of the counselee's person, he had better be wary.

To return now to the deeper aspects of the personality of the typical religious worker, can we discover any pattern by which the whole style of life can be understood? We have pointed out that this individual throws himself completely into his work according to the "all or none" law, is especially careful of details, is apt to shelve the sex problem as separate from his normal life, and exhibits an exaggerated opinion of the importance of his work.

The great care for details—and other symptoms here point in the same direction—is one of the tell-tale marks of what we term the "compulsion neurosis." Sometimes called "obsessional neurosis," this is the neurosis of the person who for some inexplicable reason feels compelled to certain detailed forms of behavior that are normally not regarded as important. Going back every morning to try the door a couple of times though one knows one has locked it, is an example of a harmless and more or less universal form of the neurosis. The person who is ridden by duty, particularly when this duty is a matter of external details, is another example. This compulsion neurosis is the typical neurosis of religious people, even the typical one of our day, according to Rank. It is often connected with premonitions of spiritual and magical punishment. The compulsion neurotic feels, in some cases, that something supernaturally terrible will happen if he does not step on every crack in the sidewalk or tap every fencepost with his cane.

We see in our typical religious worker indications of this neurosis. He must not fail in details, and to ward off doom he may believe he must dress just right or pray in a special manner, as by the pagan prayer-wheels, or go through certain routines at his office. Why is he so afraid of failing? People fail at all times, as a matter of fact, even in big things let alone small matters; to err is human; but this individual has a peculiarly strong feeling that his mistakes will bring him magical doom.

We have pointed out that the particular tension with which this individual works indicates an exaggerated ambition. It is a basic principle that neurotic ambition is connected with some deep inferiority feeling; and to be sure, we do find evidences in our typical religious worker of this inferiority feeling. It may take a moral form, the individual feeling unusual moral guilt and imperfection and therefore making strenuous efforts to compensate by ambitious striving. The root of the inferiority varies with different cases: the reader will remember that it was an inferiority feeling which led George B. to push his campaign of reform with such vigor.

No matter what the source of the inferiority, the consequent exaggerated ambition will, in the religious person, take a religious and moral form. In other words, this individual will pick the moral area for the scene of his ego's battle for supremacy. He will exhibit a "drive to be on top" morally. And he will feel special guilt when he is not on top. The "holier-than-thou" attitude is not an exception; it is merely the superiority complex which is the reverse side of the inferiority feeling. That is why persons of this type place such emphasis on moral details. The outsider can point out that the details do not make so much difference in the end, but to this individual they do make a difference—all the difference of his ego-supremacy, which is the central concern of his life. Religious and moral reformers—when their reforms do not have objective background—are to be understood in this category.

It is easy to see how some individuals can elevate themselves over other people by this technique of emphasizing petty moral and religious details. Indeed, in the case of a minister who gave up tea and coffee and cocoa we shall see that his real reason was not "to keep his body a temple of God" but to make himself better than persons around him who did indulge in the beverages. Adler discusses such a case and concludes, "it illustrates how ambition breaks into religious problems, and how vanity makes its bearer a judge over virtue, vice, purity, corruption, good and evil." [4]

Now there is a more serious aspect to this problem, an aspect more arresting to those religiously sophisticated persons who do not fit in the above categories. It is this: the religious person, to the extent that he feels inferiority and a consequent exaggerated ambition, cannot help morally judging other people. For since his ego-striving is in the moral realm, the depreciating of others morally will mean the elevating of himself. No matter how often he rebukes himself with Jesus' commandment, "Judge not," and no matter how viciously he suppresses these judgments, even deriving a certain pleasure from his refusal to "gossip," he will continue to condemn unconsciously. And unconscious judgment and condemnation of others is even more unhealthy than conscious, so that we can prefer the overt expression of an individual's opinions of another if we know he has these opinions anyway. Is there no escape from the vicious circle? Only the understanding of the ego-pattern —such as we are trying to do this very moment.

This brings us to the matter of moral judgments in counseling. It is clear, first from a Christian point of view, that no one has a right to judge another human being: the command, "judge not," is incontrovertible, particularly since it was given a dynamic by Jesus' own life. And psychotherapeutically in the second place, judging is unpermissible: "and above all," as Adler says, "let us never allow ourselves to make any *moral* judgments, judgments concerning the moral worth of a human being!" [5]

But as pointed out above it is precisely the religious counselor who finds it most difficult not to condemn. Jung holds that the reason people hesitate to confess to their minister, but go to a psychiatrist instead, is their fear that the minister will condemn. And he goes on to say, "He is never in touch when he passes judgment. . . . . We can get in touch with another person only by an attitude of unprejudiced objectivity." [6] The Freudians therefore contend that the therapist should be ethically neutral, which cuts religious people out. This does not solve the problem, however; the therapist cannot be ethically neutral; such is one of the delusions of Freudianism. The therapist—in our case the counselor—must presuppose some kind of ethical meaning, and if he refuses to do so consciously he is still doing so unconsciously, just as Freud presupposes hedonistic. deterministic ethics.

The only way out is the way of true religion, in which the counselor learns to esteem and appreciate other persons without condemning them. It is the way of understanding, of "unprejudiced objectivity"; it is the way of empathy. The ability to "judge not" is the watershed between true

176

religion and egocentric religiosity. It is supremely illustrated when one who enunciated this commandment was himself able to say, "Neither do I condemn thee."

After discussing at length these typical neurotic tendencies of religious workers, let us conclude with suggestions on the overcoming of them and, thereby, the fitting of the counselor for effective service.

In the first place, the counselor must understand the particular form this neurotic pattern takes in his own personality. The very understanding will go far toward a cure, and certainly it will illuminate for him the quirks in himself against which he must guard while counseling others. Understanding his inferiority feeling, he will see his selfish ambition in its naked form; and thereupon the neurotic aspect of his ambition will become relaxed. Let no one think that this relaxing will diminish the person's productivity and creativity. It will, in fact, give him an increased creativity; for creativity requires the spontaneity which comes from periodic relaxation, and it is blocked by the tension of strong ego-striving.

In the second place, the religious counselor should develop the *courage of imperfection*. This means the ability to fail. The individual with the compulsion neurosis who is not willing to fail must perforce fight only on a minor battlefield; no wonder he concerns himself with details, for in his own little backyard he does not risk failure. The courage of imperfection means the transferring of one's efforts to a major battlefield where significant things are done and failure or success becomes relatively incidental.

In the third place, the counselor needs to learn to *enjoy the process* of living as well as the goals. This will enable him to escape the "all or none" compulsion: for enjoying the process means responding partially, deriving enjoyment "on the wing" as one moves towards ends. **And** this enjoying of the process will relieve him from the necessity of having ulterior motives for his actions, doing this and that for the sake of some end which is outside the picture. Then he will be enabled to develop outside interests and friendships, one of the lacks our original analysis disclosed.

In the fourth place, let the counselor be sure he is *interested in people for their own sakes.* If he still believes he loves them "for God's sake" let him ask whether this "God" is not a covering for his own ego-striving; or if "for Jesus' sake," let him observe whether this cliche, too, is not an excuse for a failure to appreciate persons for and in themselves.

And this means that the would-be counselor will have to do some genuine purging of his religion, relentlessly ferreting out the false elements and expurgating them by the classical method of repentance. There is then a chance that he may be able sincerely to say, "Not my will but thine be done." When he can do this, it will be proven that the religious approach cuts the Gordian knot of the ego-bias in counseling, and that in the end the truly religious person makes the best counselor.

## Chapter IX

## MORALS AND COUNSELING

EVERY PERSONALITY problem is a moral problem. That is to say, every personality problem has ultimate moral implications; for it refers to that question which is basic to all morals, "How shall I live?" So we can expect that the healthy personality will be distinguished by its ability to negotiate the moral relations of life adequately, and we can set it down as a basic principle that a correct moral adjustment to life is the end-result of any successful counseling process.

But the mistake made by many counselors is in attempting to take a short-cut to this moral goal. Particularly if they work in the religious field, untrained counselors are apt to jump too quickly at the moral implications of the problem. And then they endeavor, often without realizing it, to pass on to the counselee a specific set of moral standards. Now it is to be granted that the counselee may need moral standards, and granted also that the counselor will possess more or less adequate standards of his own which he could pass on. But in actual practice such a procedure short-circuits the counseling process and robs the individual of his inalienable right of molding his own morality in the crucible of his own suffering and tensions.

Let us observe what happens when the counselor

makes this mistake and approaches the interview from a moralistic point of view. A minister recently described to me the case of a student who had come to him with the problem of masturbation. In counseling with this student the minister had pictured to him his future love relation-ship, marriage, and home, and had then exhorted him to keep these ideals before him and thus conquer the tempta-tion to masturbate. What would happen in this case? The student goes home, let us say, to his solitary room where he lives in somewhat lonely fashion (it is often the solitary and lonely persons who are troubled with this problem); and there he will fight the urge to masturbate by holding up before himself the image of his future home. But this image is important to him at the time only because it has become connected, through the minister's exhortation, with his temptation. And so the more he thinks of the so-called ideal the more vividly the idea of masturbation arises in his mind. Furthermore, the minister's exhortation has probably increased his guilt feeling, and consequently he feels he should hate himself and so struggles against him-self the more bitterly. Now the desire to masturbate has become stronger in this process, in fact stronger every moment he has held the idea in his mind even in the en-deavor to vanquish it. At the same time his esteem of him-self has been lowered as his guilt feelings have increased; so eventually he concludes that if he is such a depraved creature anyway he might as well give in to the urge. A vicious circle has been set up which makes the prob-lem of the young man all the worse.

One is surprised that the simple psychology of tempta-tion is not better understood among religious people. It is clear, even without profound psychological understand-ing, that most temptations are not to be conquered by a di-rect, frontal attack. This only emphasizes the temptation, and if it be a matter of desire—such as liquor or sex—the more it is emphasized the more vivid the desire becomes. Constructively speaking, the best way to remove the power of temptation is to remove the image from the center of attention. To do this the individual must become so interested in healthy pursuits that there is no attention left for the unhealthy desire. The adage has it that "an expulsive affection drives out temptations"; this is true to the extent that the affection is genuine and not merely seized upon with the ulterior purpose of using it as a weapon.

When all is said and done, the thing necessary is that the individual make a courageous, zestful, many-sided adjustment to living—and against such a healthy personality, with all its enthusiastic interests, specific temptations will have little power. This is the approach that should have been taken in the above instance. If the minister had probed below the problem on the surface, he would no doubt have found that the masturbation was merely a symptom of some deeper personality maladjustment; and he could then have helped the student to a healthy adjustment of this. Holding up the ideal of the future love and home is not in itself wrong; constructive goals do have a very important function in counseling. But the goal, or ideal, must grow out of the situation, not be merely handed down from above. It must be indigenous to the counselee, an expression of his own unique aims in line with the development of his own unique personality.

*Exhortation* should come only after *understanding*. By itself, either in preaching or counseling, exhortation accomplishes very little good and may do definite harm. It will increase the individual's guilt feeling and thus make him struggle harder but in a negative way. No doubt the student in the above example had been "trying" too hard already, for it is characteristic of persons with personality difficulties that they struggle hard but destructively. They are like fish caught in a net—the more desperately they struggle the worse they become caught. Destructive struggling causes a greater disunity in the personality, and that is exactly what we wish to avoid. To use another figure, such an indivdiual's will has become knotted up like two wrestlers who have such strong holds on each other that neither can move. No wonder the person cannot act effectively in the outside world!

We are not belittling *tension* or genuine *willing;* both of these are necessary to healthy personality. But they must be based upon understanding. Then the willing will not be a wrestling match merely on the surface of the person's mind but a reorganization of his whole personality for movement in the new direction.

For these reasons it is necessary to emphasize the principle that *the problem of the counselee should be approached as a matter of mental health, not of morality.* Then both counselor and counselee will be able to view it objectively, with a minimum of squeamishness or prudishness getting in the way. By putting aside superficial, immediate moralism, they will be fitted to arrive closer in the end to a true morality which will endure.

### CREATIVE INDIVIDUALITY IN MORALS

MORAL LIVING, like all living, begins with the individual's self-expression—expression of his passions, his instinctual drives, his desires and inner urges of every sort. Morality means self-expression in terms of structure, but the point to be emphasized here is that without the individual's self-expression there is no content to moral living. The instinctual drives of hunger and sex, the passions of anger and hate and love, the desires to have friends or to create—all of these urges and an infinite number of others furnish the material which is the content for morality. Without them there would be nothing to morality but a dry form like a river bed without any water.

We speak of these instinctual urges as surging up from the individual's unconsciousness. Freud has given us his unforgettable description of this "id," the seething cauldron out of the deep, dark unconsciousness from which emerge all sorts of instinctual urges and appetites and desires. These are typified, in Freudian terms, by libido. And Jung, we recollect, carried through the description of the unconscious to include man's hopes and fears and images and every sort of psychic content. Out of this great reservoir come the phantasies which become the great art of mankind, the creative ideas which are the embryos of philosophies, and the insights which are developed into religions.

The basic instinctual urge within the individual has been given many names by philosophers and psychologists: it is the "*elan vital*" or vital impulse of Bergson, the "Will" of Nietzsche and Schopenhauer, the "creative impulse," etc. But whatever the name, we are here dealing with the inner, irrational urges which give content to man's living. This is the creative flow, the stream of life which rises internally like an artesian well and pours out its living waters.

The content furnished by the instinctual urges is both good and evil. The "good" is to be defined as instinctual urges which are directed in socially constructive ways. But by themselves the urges are more egocentric and antisocial than good. They are irrational, furthermore, and rebel against direction; they are like horses which still have some wildness in them, straining at the bit.

People are frightened by this instinctual side of their lives. They recognize something dangerous in the urges rising within them and impelling them to love and to hate, to make sexual conquest and to fight, to seize the world in ambition and force themselves into ascendancy over other people. There is some of the Faust in each of us—the urge to master whole worlds, to express our will-to-live without limit—and it terrorizes us. In these powerful urges we sense tendencies toward destruction of ourselves as well as destruction of others.

Modern man naturally hates to admit the existence of these urges, many of which are definitely antisocial and would create havoc in any community if they were once allowed expression. He is chagrined to realize that he possesses, and is possessed of, many more powerful irrational impulses than his self-respect would like; he is much more of a raging animal, in Freud's terms, than he would wish. And so he may seek to repress the instinctual side of his personality. He would prefer not to admit the instinctual urges into consciousness at all, but that way out is denied him except by the detour of neurosis. Therefore he takes what appears to be the next best method, the endeavor to control his urges by superficial willing, by strengthening his super-ego and placing it like a powerful guard at the outlet of his id. Protestantism in particular has tended in this direction—tended, that is, to assume that the issues of life can be settled in the sphere of immediate, conscious decision. Thus we speak of "mastering life" and "conquering one's self." We sign a card or make a public statement and assume the matter is settled.

After realizing that outright repression will not work, people tend to set up systems of rules by which they can control their instinctual urges. The more frightened they are of their urges, the more static these rules become. They may devise a detailed system of inflexible principles which they can apply in mechanical fashion to every situation. Adler speaks pointedly of these "people who attempt to pigeon-hole every activity and every event according to some principle which they have assumed valid for every situation. . . . . We have the impression that they feel themselves so insecure that they must squeeze all of life and living into a few rules and formulae, lest they become too frightened of it. Faced with a situation for which they have no rule or formulae, they can only run away." [1] This rule-making relieves such people of the difficult responsibility of making new decisions.

People have a right to be afraid of their instinctual urges. For therein lie dangerous potentialities for evil as well as possibilities for creative good. But their mistake is in taking short-cuts; the techniques of repression, simple inhibition, and rule-making simply will not work. Man cannot get the better of these powerful forces in the unconscious by dishonesty. He may succeed in being respectable and circumspect and never overstep his rules in his community, but then he suddenly throws himself into a war which spreads hate and murder over continents until whole countries are red with blood. Or he may be perfectly moral in his own personal life but create such poison in his surroundings by his repressions that his children are turned into the world semi-neurotic.

Even in the case of the individual by himself, it is clear that direct "fighting" of the unconscious urges will not work. Here is John Doe, for example, a man who attempts to guide himself by detailed rules and resolutions. He resolves this or that thing in his conscious mind and then holds to the resolution with a tenacity which we unfortunately call "will power." But it is the forces from deeper levels of unconsciousness which have most to do with John Doe's or anybody else's behavior. And if his resolution is made without reference to these deeper tendencies, we can be sure it will ultimately be "steam-rollered." Then

185

Mr. Doe wonders why, no matter how hard he consciously tries, he cannot keep his resolution. As a matter of fact the very resolution Mr. Doe has made may incite a compensatory process in his unconscious which, when it finally bursts forth, will cause him to swing back to the opposite extreme.

What we need is *cooperation* between instinctual urges and conscious aims. If there is mainly antagonism between them, there results a greater and greater separation of the conscious portion from the unconscious bulk of the personality, and this works directly against mental health. The ideal situation is that the rider (the conscious ego, in Freud's phrase) intelligently guide the horses (the forces from the id). Such a relationship of cooperation is possible only on the basis of understanding and reconciliation. It means that the individual must above all be *honest* with his instinctual urges. Then his willing will not be a private wrestling match on the limited surface of consciousness, but a reorganization of more nearly the whole man. Instead of merely *making resolutions*, he will *become resolved*. His decisions, backed by forces from the "profound and powerful depths," will then have power and effectiveness.

All the good we have in life, it has been said, has its source in these instinctual urges as well as the evil. Love springs up as well as hate. The emotions which make possible cooperation and service are found here. Sexuality, for example, has wrecked many a life; but it has also led to the creation of families and great loves. The anger that surges up in us can be used to attack evils and result in great humanitarian reforms. And so the man who turns roughly against his instinctual life may succeed temporarily in avoiding evil, but he has also blocked off his possibilities for doing good. He who cannot hate, said Emerson, cannot

186

**love.** The individual who tries to dry up his instinctual urges has robbed his life of content; his river is dry. So, even if we could repress this dark and unruly side of our natures, we would not want to. We should have got rid of our chaff, but we should find ourselves also without wheat.

Life is therefore a much more portentous affair than our little systems admit. We men are not the petty beings which our morality of mere "effort" implies. Within us are tremendous potentialities for good and evil. Man can build great civilizations. And he can then wreck them with such violence that there is naught left but blood and smoldering ruins. Man will let himself be killed for love or hate, and he will kill others for the same reasons. Man can let his personality dissipate until he scarce can be distinquished from the animals, yet he can develop his mind till his "thoughts go wandering through eternity," and he can loose his creative phantasies until he makes delicate Gothic spires that in sheer beauty rank with the creations of God himself. The war in Spain is man's doing, but so is the culture of Greece. For centuries man has marched in armies, but for as many centuries he has tilled the soil and watched the plants come up in the spring and fed his fellows with the fruits of the land. Yes, infinite potentialities for good and evil—such is man. Life is not a matter for simple optimism—for there is evil; nor for mere pessimism—for there is good. The possibility for good in the face of evil is what gives life tragic meaning.

Our attitude toward our instinctive urges should be, then, not one of conflict and repression, but rather one of understanding and cooperation, aiming toward the utilization of these forces for good. This takes courage, for it means looking below the superficial and petty moral rules in the interests of a more meaningful morality in the end.

A counselor related to me the story of Janice D., an

attractive college girl who had become filled with a general dissatisfaction toward herself and her living. A talented and artistic girl, she had come from a well-to-do family and had begun her college career in a respectable manner by joining her mother's sorority and settling down to a major in classics. It was during her sophomore year that she came to the counselor to discuss her newly found "universal religion," which appeared to consist of the belief that "everything that is, is right." Then Janice suddenly announced that she was about to resign her position on the church student cabinet and go out on a "big drunk." The counselor discovered that the girl, suffering from an accumulation of tensions within her personality which took the form of a great desire to burst the bonds of her traditional living, had gone to a faculty member for counsel and had been advised to find some suitable man with whom to have periodic sexual relations. Janice did get drunk, was promptly dismissed from her sorority and escaped expulsion from college only because of the efforts of an understanding dean.

Now the counselor in this case was in a difficult position. If she had become frightened and implored Janice to control and repress her rebellious impulses, she would have found herself cut off immediately from the opportunity to help. But fortunately she was intelligent and courageous; and even though she was unable to save the girl from the "detour" of getting drunk, she did retain an influence in the situation. Janice did not carry out the sex suggestion—which was fortunate, for mere sexual expression, entered into for its own sake in casual and random fashion, cannot help anyone solve a personality problem and may make matters much worse.

After her spree Janice attained equilibrium. She shifted her course from classics to sociology and devoted herself to a worth-while and satisfying college life. She is now doing graduate work in sociology and appears to be on the road to a constructive and useful maturity.

What was the significance of this "fling" in Janice's life? Let us notice, first, that it was connected with a change to a *life-affirming religion*. This was probably not a true religion, in any final sense; but it did represent her naive attempt to affirm the universe. Her change from classics, a relatively formal subject, to sociology represents the same movement toward the affirming of real life. The getting drunk, thirdly, is a grasp at reality on the sensuous level. This fling, then, appears to represent Janice's birth throes in her development from formalization to vitality. She was declaring her right to live; this was her war of independence by which she sought the right to fly the flag of her own individual autonomy, all of which unavoidably involved an element of rebellion.

The tendency of most counselors would be to repress such a fling in their counselees, for they well recognize the danger involved. But clearly Janice had this fling in her system, so to speak; and it had to come out in some form if she was ever to become an autonomous individual. The counselor's function, then, was not to forbid the expression, but as much as possible *to direct it into creative* channels. In Janice's case the revolt from classics to sociology was, we may assume, a creative step. The revolt to her new religion contained creative elements, which she could retain when she returned to a sounder religious point of view. If the counselor could have substituted a more creative activity for the getting drunk, so much the better. This being impossible, as it seemed to be, the counselor's aim would be to make this action as little destructive as possible.

It not infrequently happens that students, surfeited

with subjective academic pursuits, find it necessary to rebel against something. The counselor cannot tell them not to fight, but he can tell them *what* to fight. And there are plenty of evils the fighting of which will furnish William James's "moral equivalent" of getting drunk. Probably it is true that every youth arrives at a stage in his life when he must rebel, have his fling, declare himself autonomous even though it costs him and others pain. We adults should not be too frightened at this. It is the sign of vitality, power, potentiality; it is proof of the creative flow of instinctual urges. If adults persuade repression, they may do more harm than good. But adult counselors can suggest channels of expression. Youth must sow its oats, but they need not be *wild* oats. So let them sow, but let the oats in their bags be used for *good*. And here is where the courageous counselor can help.

We have been speaking of the instinctual urges which surge up within the individual, and we have stated that the content of living—including *moral* living—is furnished by the expression of these urges. The person who has attained this healthy self-expression exhibits certain characteristics which we shall now describe.

*Spontaneity* is the most obvious characteristic of the person who has learned self-expression. Spontaneity is prized as a virtue because it indicates that the individual has integrated the deeper levels of his personality; he has achieved some unity between unconscious urges and his conscious aims, and therefore he does not need always to "think twice before he speaks." He has come to terms with his instinctual life, and so he is relieved of the necessity of always being on guard for fear he will do something or say something he will later regret. The spontaneous person acts with more of his whole self. The mere fact that he can do this proves that he has attained a high degree of personality health. The individual, on the other hand, who has not come to terms with his instinctual life, who is always at sharp war with himself, cannot afford to be spontaneous for fear some wild dog will leap out of his unconscious depths and ruin his reputation on the spot. We may rightly suspect, therefore, that he who is always carefully controlling himself in speech and action actually does have particularly antisocial tendencies which he has to keep covered up.

*Genuineness* is another characteristic of the person who has learned healthy self-expression. Genuineness means speaking and living from the depths of one's personality; people call this showing one's "real self" to the world, which actually means, again, showing more of one's *whole self*. We all resent other people being ungenuine in our presence, for we have the impression that their actions and words do not tap any deep level of their being. We have the impression that if such a person were given chloroform, his unconscious mumblings would be quite the opposite of the conscious compliments he is paying us, or that when he goes home and lets down the artificial props, he will proceed to tell his wife what scoundrels he really thinks we are. Spontaneity and genuineness, when all is said and done, are only forms of elementary honesty. He who can be honest has learned the secret of personality health. *Speaking, acting, living from the depths of one's whole self*—this is the ideal.

Another important characteristic of the self-expressive person is *originality*. Every individual is unique, different from every self that has been, is, or will be in the world. When he achieves his own unique selfhood he becomes autonomous, an original self directed from within. This gives him originality. His reactions have a certain newness; he moves through life like a fresh breeze of creativity

He has escaped the static, life-thwarting strait-jacket of the systems of external rules; and he tends to become more and more dynamic. We cannot expect to measure him by the artificial, standardized yardstick of consistency. For nothing is consistent in this life anyway—every situation is different from every other, and every person is different today from what he was yesterday. Thus the individual who has achieved his originality is able better to meet the ever-changing situations of life. He has become part of the infinite creativity of the life-process, and it is expressed in the unique creativity of his own self. His living surges up from within; this it is that gives strength and convincingness to his personality.

It follows that *freedom* is a special characteristic of the individual who has come to terms with his instinctual urges. One cannot be free, of course, while his consciousness is locked in warfare with tendencies from his unconsciousness. That is why the aim of psychotherapeutic treatment is often summed up as setting the individual free —free from special inhibitions and repressions, from childhood fixations, from training formulae, and so on. Counselors likewise aim to help the person become free. People need to be freed; one feels great pity for the great majority of people that they should be so enslaved by unnecessary fears. One sees them going through life carrying great psychological burdens which keep them from freedom even more really than the prisoner's iron ball-and-chain. It is a truism that most people develop to only a third or less of their personality possibilities. The counselor will aim to set people free so that they can develop into their own unique, autonomous selves and realize some of the rich, untapped potentialities in their personalities.

To live the life of self-expression requires courage. To love greatly, to admit one's hate without having it destroy one's equilibrium, to express anger, to rise to heights of joy and to know deep sorrow, to go on far adventures in spite of loneliness, to catch lofty ideas and carry them into action—in short, to live out the infinite number of instinctual urges that rise in glorious challenge within one —this requires courage. Yet we must not hold back out of cowardice. We must have the courage to overcome petty inhibitions, to move ahead in spite of all our little worries, to triumph over the burden of unnecessary fears. People are inclined to hold back, for they know the way ahead is lined with dangers. But this holding back is often the beginning of their personality problems—for the stream of life will not be dammed. The counselor must give people courage to live. It is his function to help them overcome the little fears, the dread of meeting people, the fear of falling in love, the anxieties that may seize them on taking a new job. What a great proportion of the anxieties that attack people are unnecessary and useless! There is reason for the deep anxiety inherent in the tragic possibilities of living, as will be discussed below; but the infinite number of little fears and worries each day simply hold people back from creative living. But human beings cannot stagnate; they must move on, for there is great good ahead as well as possibilities of evil.

Yes, the artesian wells within the individual must not be stopped up—the stream of life, with all its instinctual impulsions and emotional colors must flow on. It is the counselor's aim to give people, who come to him broken in courage, a glimpse of the great possibilities ahead for joy and achievement. So many interesting things to do —so many friends to be made—so many new places to visit, new things to learn—so many deeds of service waiting to be done! From this point of view the great prophets of the life of self-expression are right: Rousseau when he cries, "Ah! to live must be a beautiful thing!"[2] and calls on men to live themselves out to the full. And Nietzsche, when he rightly charges that " 'virtue,' in my opinion, has been *more* injured by the *tediousness* of its advocates than by anything else,"[3] and challenges men to be "free spirits" and to express themselves heroically as "supermen."

## STRUCTURE IN MORALITY

IN THE ABOVE section we have been emphasizing the value of instinctual self-expression. But self-expression by itself is not enough. It represents the beginning, but only the first half, of the problem of moral living. It furnishes the content to morality, but this content requires *structure*. The mere content without the structure would be like a river without any banks—the water would flow in every direction and waste itself on the sands. We now consider, then, the other aspect of every moral system, the structure: the limiting, guiding, controlling factor which, like the banks of a river, will direct the instinctual expression into the right channels.

It is very significant that self-expression, by itself, ends in self-destruction. Take Nietzsche, for example, one of the greatest trumpeters of the glories of instinctual self-expression in all history; his "superman" would climb "beyond good and evil" to the very pinnacle of triumphant expression of his own will to power. Nothing could stand in his way—neither society, nor despicable "herd morality," nor the "cowardly Christian moral system." But Nietzsche, trying to live in this way, was a heroic tragedy; he could not get along with other people and was desperately lonely; he was neurotic most of his life and died psychotic. Or take Rousseau. This singer of the beauties of self-development also failed in his personal relationships; he finally married a waitress and put his children in a foundling home. It is not that Nietzsche and Rousseau are wrong. It is that they have only half the truth. They have the content of life—and here they have much to teach us—but not the structure. The psychotherapeutic view of morals, particularly in its Freudian aspects, tends likewise to over-emphasize instinctual forces and to undervalue the structure of moral living.

How are we to find this necessary structure? First, in the *norms of social living.* The person who sets out to express his impulses by caprice soon finds himself colliding with other persons, and he learns by painful experience that it is necessary to direct his expression into certain channels set up by the conditions of social living. Alfred Adler has best understood the implications of the social structure of life. Since every individual is dependent upon other people for birth and growth, for food and shelter and protection, for love and companionship, there is set up a great web of interdependence among people. Thus the individual, Adler points out, owes a constant debt to society. He is responsible to his group, and if he does not learn to cooperate he is destroyed. A man cannot violate this "love and logic which bind us all together" without dire consequences to his personality health. Pronounced egocentricity (the opposite of social interest) leads to neurosis, and the individual becomes healthy again only when he renounces this egocentricity in favor of a greater interest in the well-being of the total group. "All that we demand of a human being and the highest praise we can give him, is that he should be a good fellow worker, a friend to all other men, and a true partner in love and marriage. If we are to put it in a word, we may say that he should prove himself a fellow man." [4]

This is to say that unselfishness and cooperation are inherent in the very laws of social living. This is the

sociological proof for the Christian concept of brother-
hood; but it does not, of course, go as far as the Christian
concept of love. The Adlerian social structure is only a
partial answer; if we were to stop here, it would appear
that the channel of morality were merely the conventions
of society which demand a "cheap adjustment." No, the
social structure must be viewed as one aspect of something
much deeper and broader.

Our next and more profound approach to a moral
structure is through the *moral archetypes*. This is "inborn
morality," the moral patterns which we have because we
are born as men, the "inherited pathways" of which Jung
speaks so often. We may think of this as humanity's psychic depository of morality, consisting of various moral
patterns that have their seat in the very roots of man's
being and are passed on through age after age in the collective unconsciousness of mankind. This is an inner approach to morality—it means that one can look into his own
depths and there discover the faint outlines of a moral
structure. Specific morals always owe most of their form
to the particular culture in which they developed, but
these archetypes reach down to a level below the varying
cultures of mankind and hence have a claim to universality.
This explains why similar moral ideas spring up in different parts of the world in races and cultures that have
had no contact with each other. For an example let us
cite the prohibition of incest, prevailing in practically all
primitive tribes and coming into classical expression in the
Oedipus myth. Or the rudimentary respect for human
life that comes out in prohibition of murder within the
group. Or the demand for justice, the "balancing" of human relationships, which crops up in every culture. These
are expressions of moral archetypes which help form the
structure of man's morality.

The great geniuses of goodness—Jesus, St. Francis, and the long line of them—are those who penetrate through the depths of their own unconsciousness into the collective unconsciousness of mankind and there tap the universal archetypes. Their expressions of these archetypes become the classics of morality. Many modern psychologists have said that the statement, "He who seeks to save his life will lose it," represents a basic truth rediscovered by modern psychology. Men all over the world would recognize in this moral statement something which applied to them. Take the Sermon on the Mount to oriental India, for example; and Gandhi will tell you it is his deepest moral insights coming back, as it were, to him. That is why the precepts of the Sermon on the Mount stand out as moral classics, true century after century; there is certainly something here that comes from the deepest structure of life. It is the essential world speaking to us. We rightly call it revelation, and the Revealer the greatest of the prophets; for he is the channel through which the profoundest meaning of life breaks upon us. When one turns into his own soul and asks the troubled question, "How should I live?" he finds Jesus' answers as the clearest expression of the essence of his own being.

There is difficulty, of course, in making this concept of moral archetypes distinct and understandable. For the archetypes arise in the abysmal depths in our being in which the indistinct merges into the unknown. And let us grant that specific mores as we find them in conventional society may or may not have any connection with basic archetypes. Most specific morals owe their form to the particular culture they were made to serve. There is a danger that any inconsequential convention, such as not playing baseball on Sunday, may be said by certain groups to be an eternal archetype, so that thereupon they have an excuse for compelling everyone else to conform. The archetypes do not have to do with *specific* details; they are rather expressions of deep principles which come out of the very structure of man's life.

Do we have so far—that is, in social living and in the moral archetypes—the adequate structure for morality for which we have been searching? No, these are only partial and incomplete; we need to arrive at a more objective structure, stronger "banks" to serve to channel the powerful forces of man's instinctual urges. The inadequacy of the archetypes as a final structure can be seen in the morality of Nazi Germany. There we observe a very definite structure arising out of the collective unconscious of the German race, a Nordic, Teutonic morality which is surprisingly successful at freeing and channeling the instinctual forces *within* the group. But this success is bought at the price of loosing tremendously demonic and destructive forces against those *outside* the group. The Nazi structure is partial and therefore must rest upon hate and venom and demonry. We need an *objective universality* in our moral structure.

The Adlerian social norm is inadequate by itself. For though man knows he should cooperate, he ordinarily does not do so until he is forced to; he knows that if everyone ran through the red light, traffic would be destroyed, but yet he will often drive through if there is no policeman in sight. Man knows he should not kill, but yet he does. Adler seemed to think that man *can* cooperate simply when he understands that it is best for him to do so. But morality is not so easy as this. There is a contradiction within man between his will to selfish power and his social interest; and though "ought" is on the side of the latter, man has a tendency to follow the former. Freud was more profound when he saw this basic contradiction in man; he held that man is composed of two contradictory impulses, that of "eros" or love—which tends to unite living substances and build up—and "aggressiveness" or the death instinct—which tends to attack and destroy. So if man is to cooperate and live as a social being, says Freud, he must be compelled against his own desires by the harsh laws of culture.

This contradiction within man is of extreme importance in morality. St. Paul sees it when he says to the Romans, "The good which I would I do not; but the evil which I would not, that I practice," the reason for this being the "sin which dwelleth in me." All through history men have feared the instinctual drives, for they contain demonic forces which burst over the banks of "oughtness." An individual knows, for example, that if all men had sexual relations outside marriage our social situation would be destroyed; yet this act often takes place, and even at times against the better judgment of the persons concerned. No wonder the Greeks identified sin with physical sensuality. But the contradiction within man is not simply a matter of sensual desires; it takes the more important form of will to power, the drive to dominate others and to elevate one's self. Arrogance and pride are more the roots of man's immorality and sin than mere sensuality.

However one views it, it is clear that this contradiction in man's nature makes moral living an extremely difficult achievement. Suppose we define a moral act as one which is unselfish in motivation, i.e., non-egocentric. Now if an individual "wills" to do an unselfish act, his very willing will undoubtedly have egocentric motives; and therefore the act will not really be unselfish. Seeing how difficult it is for man really to do good, St. Paul and Augustine and others have concluded that it is impossible to do good without God's aid. And in the light of these considerations Christian theology has developed the doctrine of original sin. It means to say, simply, that this contradiction exists within man, and therefore he tends to sin in every act.

Hence man's moral problem is a serious one, and no simple structure will be adequate. The river of instinctual forces will overflow and destroy weak banks of social norms or the indefinite and partial channel of archetypes.

The only adequate structure for morality is that based upon the *ultimate meaning of life*. Such a structure will be universal. It will possess objectivity, for it will be outside the individual as well as in his own mind. It will be an archetype of the universe, so to speak, rather than simply that found in mankind's collective unconsciousness. All other partial structures will be included and transcended in this universal frame. From it we shall get norms for acting which are rooted in the ultimate meaning of life.

Where is such a universal structure to be found? As a matter of fact, every individual implies in all his actions some sort of structure based upon his belief in ultimate meaning, even though he has never taken the trouble to understand it. But people have different concepts of life's ultimate meaning; hence we must decide on the most adequate concept upon which to base our morality.

In the New Testament this universal structure is called "logos," a term taken from Hellenistic philosophy meaning the "reasonable, meaningful structure of life." The memorable passage opening the Gospel of John classically explains this: "In the beginning was the Word," or to use Moffatt's more accurate translation, "The Logos existed in the very beginning, the Logos was with God, the Logos was divine . . . . through him all existence came into being. . . . . In him life lay, and this life was the Light for men: amid the darkness the Light shone." This Logos, which we can term the mind of God, is in the world from the beginning, yet it comes in special form in the person of Christ.

So the ultimate structure is the nature of God. The principles of God are the principles which underlie life from the beginning of creation to the end. It is with this meaningful structure that human living must be brought into accord. This is the form which gives the ultimate and universal channel for human instinctual expression.

That is why Jesus' moral statements strike us as having eternal truth—he was the Logos, the very mind of God speaking to man. Take Jesus' law of love, for example: "Love your enemies" and "Love your neighbor as yourself." We feel spontaneously that this is the perfect form of love, and therefore the will of God in regard to our instinctual self-expression.

Yes, we recognize this absolute love commandment as the will of God, yet we do not live up to it. And that is precisely what the contradiction within man means. It is the contradiction between his natural egocentricity and the demands which the structure makes upon him. On the one hand man knows that he should be unselfish, should love others as much as himself—this is God speaking to him. But on the other hand, he does not do it. The mere fact that man can recognize the commandments of God proves that he has a certain deep point of connection with God. For he was created "in God's image" and participates in the divine structure we term logos; he is a son of God, though now far from home, so to speak. This good, original form of man is his *essential* nature. The absolute command, "Love your enemies," makes a reflection in man and is not altogether foreign; but no matter how hard man tries, he can live up to it only very imperfectly in this imperfect world. Thus we see another aspect of the contradiction: namely, between *what man is and what he ought to be*.

How did this contradiction arise? The Biblical story of the fall is the classical attempt at explanation. We see in this story the idea that man was originally created "good"; he was, that is, an image of God. This constitutes the *essential* aspect of man's nature. At that moment he was not at conflict with himself and therefore had no moral consciousness. An enviable state, some weary persons may conjecture! But sin entered, the story continues, to disturb this original unity, in the form of Adam's disobedience to God. Hence man *existentially* is "fallen." He possesses in his nature the image of God, but it is at all times in conflict with his self-will and egocentricity. With this split in man's nature came "knowledge of good and evil," i.e., moral consciousness and struggle. The details of the story should not be pressed; rather, it should be viewed as an endeavor to explain why man contains the contradiction. It is not to be considered a historical or chronological matter. In fact, man is always "falling"; Adam and Christ hold a tension within every individual in every decision.

The contradiction within man thus is between his essential nature, his "God-basis," and his present state of egocentricity. It is between his willing to be in accord with God's will and his willing according to his own egocentricity. But the will of God is present, speaking to him from the very basis of his personality, like a voice from one's far home. This is the root of conscience. Socrates illustrates this with his "inner voice" which gave him guidance as to the way he should go. Conscience is our perception of the structure as it throws light into the darkness of our chaotic impulses; conscience is our glimpse of the "ought" over against our present imperfect condition. Herein is the seat of the great categorical moral imperative, the eternal "Do" or "Do not" which comes in some form to all men.

This, then, is our solution to the moral problem: *instinctual self-expression through universal structure*, which is God. The former furnishes the content, the flowing water; and the latter is the form, the banks of the river which direct the flow.

At this point we must add to our imperfect simile. For God works in man in much more intimate ways than merely directing his flow from the outside like the river-bank. The structure makes itself felt within the individual, through the archetypes and through the individual's personal contact with the will of God by means of such phenomena as conscience. Thus the action of God in the individual's life is to purify the water within the stream—to amplify our original simile—and to strengthen certain currents. This is understandable when it is remembered that the logos is a living part of each individual man; it is his essential nature, and through this man is able to hear and respond when "deep calls unto deep."

But this is no easy or simple solution to the moral problem. Man has freedom, and hence he is not forced to live according to the structure. In fact, such is his egocentricity that it is very difficult for him to do so. If he wills to be unselfish, as has been said above, his very willing will have selfish motives and hence will still be egocentric. How can man overcome this egocentric bias of his will—the deadly original sin with which he is fettered? Certainly not by mere moral effort. Rather, by giving up and responding to the demands of the structure. "For whosoever would save his life shall lose it; and whosoever shall lose his life for my sake and the gospel's shall save it." This is a process of giving one's self up and of being able thereby to answer God's call in action. Theology terms this the grace of God working in man. Paul and Augustine and a long line of Christian thinkers have concluded that the ability to do good—to transcend one's egocentric will—comes to man not by his own efforts but by God's grace. After this clarification, as Kunkel would term it, man is able to give alms without letting the "left hand know what the right hand doeth."

When the individual realizes his relation to the ultimate structure, the contradition within him is to an extent overcome. He is then able to move ahead and express his instinctual urges courageously. "Love God and do what you will" is significantly true. "To them that love God all things work together for good." When this relationship to God is made, the individual is freed from the rules and precepts and moral laws that thwart the creativity of so many people. He has transcended the law, in Paul's phrase, and lives thereafter by the creative spirit.

This acting in harmony with the structure is not static, but dynamic and ever new, for it is a matter of the individual making contact with the ever active will of God. Persons who think they can reduce the moral life to static rules have really not arrived at the ultimate structure at all, but have instead set up their own structures. This is what Jesus tried to point out to the Pharisees: "Woe unto you, scribes and Pharisees, hypocrites! for ye tithe mint and anise and cummin, and have left undone the weightier matters of the law, justice, and mercy, and faith: but these ye ought to have done, and not to have left the other undone." Like the Pharisees, we modern people feel insecure in our moral lives, and so we try to construct a calculable system which all can read as they run. But Jesus will have none of calculations. He rebukes those uncourageous persons who want sure proof: "An evil and adulterous generation seeketh after a sign."

The irony of the matter is that making the structure static in the form of external moral details destroys the real meaning of morality: "And ye have made void the word of God because of your tradition." A freshman who once counseled with me complained of loneliness. In answer to my question as to whether he had made friends with the other fellows on his floor in the dormitory, he answered, "No, I don't like them because they smoke and swear." This is a typical example of external sometime "moral" details getting in the way of human contact, and in fact blocking the possibility of love between the individual and his fellow men. This does not imply that one ought not to be discriminating in one's choice of friends, but it does imply that the discrimination should be based upon inner and more fundamental factors than in the above case. We must not make a strait-jacket out of our moral structure.

The moral system arrived at in this chapter is not intended to deal in particulars or to furnish specific answers. It is meant rather as a basic frame of reference. The specific application will vary not only with different individuals, but in every different instance with the same individual. Love is often expressed, for example, by kindness; but sometimes its best expression requires the giving of pain, and he who has frozen this commandment into a rule of kindness has lost the meaning of love. Every moral act will have something new, something creative, something unique and plastic about it. Morality is an intimately personal matter—the personalities of the individual, of God, and of other people all entering in; and consequently there are an infinite number of variables in every situation. This shows that in the long last no one can legislate morality for anyone else. We can only insist that the individual include both foci in his living: his own self-expression on one hand, and the universal structure on the other—and beyond that he must make his own creative solution. This indicates also the inadequacy of many social conventions. They often represent frozen externalizations of a principle that is far removed from the basic structure, and thus they may militate directly against true morality. The great geniuses of goodness have often found themselves in opposition to the petty social conventions of their day precisely because they saw more profoundly into the meaning of the structure. When our morality becomes truly creative, our traditions will no longer transgress the commandments of God, and the law itself will be fulfilled.

The counselor, then, will assist the counselee to find for himself this basic, creative morality. To do this it may be necessary, first, to help him overcome inhibitions and suppressions and petty fears, and in general to break down the dams of his instinctual life. But in the second place the counselor will assist him to arrive at an adequate channeling for his instinctual urges, which will be the will of God for him. And it will not be a matter of the counselor's imposing his particular moral system upon the other, for the will of God is unique for every individual. So released, the counselee will be able to develop his potentialities. His freed creative phantasy can serve good actions, can play with possibilities until he finds, in the infinite variety of alternative combinations, the adjustment which will be most fructifying in a given situation. Then his conscience will not be a petty and superficial censor serving to inhibit his development, but an instrument of insight into the universal structure of goodness.

## Chapter X

# RELIGION AND MENTAL HEALTH

### NEUROTIC RELIGION

HAROLD K. was a young minister, just graduated from the seminary and now in the process of settling down in his first parish. He was planning to be married within a few months, but he was afraid the marriage would have to be postponed because of his poor health. He feared a complete nervous breakdown. In fact he was already on the verge of it; he was so nervous that it was difficult for him to continue his church work, and his friends had advised him to give up the parish and take a complete rest for a few months.

Harold K. said his nervousness came from his continual worrying. He could not stop worrying—that was the problem he brought to the counselor. He had tried to "beat down" this worrying, to use his own very descriptive term; but his efforts had been to no avail. An inferiority "complex" had also troubled him for a number of years. He felt inferior, he said, to everyone with whom he talked.

As counselor, I noticed that his body was thin, his complexion very sallow, his eyes faded and flighty; and I observed that he did not sit still but fidgeted about continually. Another sign of nervousness was his habit of changing the subject abruptly. He spoke of the girl whom he was about to marry as a good church organist and a Sunday school teacher of long experience. The chief motive in his choice of her appeared to be her suitability as a minister's wife and a helper in the church work.

He could not understand why he should be in poor health, for he took very good care of his body. He emphasized the fact that he had given up smoking while in college, then coffee and tea, and had just recently added cocoa to the list of his renunciations. He had renounced smoking and these beverages, he said, because of his ideal of keeping his body the "temple of God." During college he had also given up card playing, dancing, and swearing in order not "to lower his ideals and go the way of the other fellows who did these things." He had always been particularly discriminating about people with whom he associated, and in his present parish he was careful not to be seen on the street with women who were not "respectable." He appeared unusually anxious to retain the respect of the people of his town. The young people of the town danced and played cards, he said; and when they asked him why he thought these things sinful, he only answered that dancing was a sin for him, but, "I can't say what it is for you; you may be strong enough to do it."

What is wrong with Harold K.?

He is already in the process of a nervous breakdown. If he had not told us that, we could have predicted it; for the elements in the style of life described above would lead inevitably to such a personality crisis. He was right in stressing his inferiority feeling; we observe that his style of life is constructed around a basic feeling of insecurity, an insecurity so strong that he must strive morally and religiously to compensate for it, and those efforts failing, finally take refuge in a nervous breakdown. There is no question that his renunciations, going so far as abstinence from tea, coffee, and cocoa, are not actually for the legitimate ideal of keeping his body at its best, but rather for the purpose of raising his own prestige above that of the persons around him. He has told us in so many words that this was his technique in making himself superior to his college fellows. And it is now his way of triumphing over the other persons in his town. This basic feeling of insecurity, for which he is striving to compensate, is evidenced in his great desire to be respected; inwardly he probably feels that he is not respectable. He is even using his marriage as a rung in this ladder of egocentricity by which he climbs to moral and religious triumph. If his fiancee's ability to fit in as a minister's wife is his chief motive in marrying her, as we have reason to assume, he is actually not marrying her for herself but for what she can do to further his own success. Such a selfish motive can lead only to failure in the marriage.

Here is a clear picture of an egocentric style of life, founded on an accentuated feeling of insecurity for which the individual attempts to compensate by religious and moral techniques. Of course the techniques will not succeed for very long. Such a style of life can lead only to neurotic crisis, and we are not surprised at Harold K.'s breakdown.

Some persons, observing how he was using religion to bolster his egocentric style of life, would advise Harold K. to throw religion out of his life altogether. As a matter of fact, this might do some good. For in getting rid of his present false religion, Harold K. would be forced ultimately to take on some elements of true religion. The counselor, however, would proceed, not by this crude method, but by helping him to understand his basic inferiority feeling which drives him to his senseless moral and religious competition; and on the basis of this understanding, Harold K. would be enabled to transform his present egocentric religion into a genuinely unselfish one. In any case, it is clear that a true religion would get him over his difficulties. It would give him deep security and genuine courage. Thus being freed of the need *to* pit his ego against other people, he would be enabled to devote himself genuinely to the service of God and his fellow men.

Using Harold K.'s case as a basis, let us pick out some tests by which we can discover and guard against the neurotic tendencies in religious living. We observe, first, that Harold K.'s religion served as a barrier between him and other people; indeed, its *raison d'etre* was the forming of this barrier. But religion should connect, should strengthen the fundamental human bond even though it accentuate differences on the surface; this inheres in the nature of love. Great religious teachers, though they have often been forced to break with the superficial demands of the society in which they lived, have emphasized their deep, basic attachment to their fellow men. We may conclude, therefore, that religion has a dangerous neurotic tendency whenever it *separates one from, rather than strengthening one's attachment to, one's fellow men.*

We observe in the second place that Harold K.'s religion did not appeal to his courage but to his cowardice. It was the instrument by which his ego attempted to attain a false security. Now there is nothing to be disparaged in religion's allaying the feeling of insecurity; indeed, to give the individual *true* security is one of the basic functions of religion, as will be explained below. But the dangerous tendency is that religious individuals, like Harold K., endeavor to gain that security by short-cuts; namely, the detailed abstensions, which lead only into the woods of illusion and never arrive back on the road of true security at all. Harold K.'s religion was too closely connected with his inferiority feeling. And thus, being an instrument primarily for meeting weakness, it ensconced him in his state of dependence and immaturity. So it can be concluded, in the second place, that religion tends to become neurotic whenever *it appeals to one's cowardice more than to one's courage.*

And finally, in the case of Harold K. where was the "life abundant"? His life was cramped, cold, frightened. What joy he got was in his egoistic triumph over others; he was already in the first stages of a nervous breakdown, nature's final stamp of disapproval upon a way of life. Indeed, his life was the opposite to the life abundant. It is not to be implied, of course, that religion turns one loose to partake of all sensuous pleasures; but religion should give one zest in living, a sense of adventure, and ability to enjoy the pleasures of human association and nature—in short, the simple, calm, and unselfish joys based on trust in God, which He who described the life abundant appreciated. And here is where Harold K. failed most miserably. Without going into detail about religious and secular pleasures, we may conclude simply that religion becomes neurotic whenever *it cramps and impoverishes life, thus destroying the possibility of living abundantly.*

That Harold K.'s case represents a misunderstanding and misuse of religion we do not need to dwell upon. One has only to read a few sentences from the recorded words of the Nazarene to discover how foreign all of this is to genuinely Christian religion.

Observing how neurotic individuals often take to religion, some psychotherapists, notably Freud, have concluded that religion itself abets mental ill health. Religion is a means, says Freud, by which man ensconces himself in a childlike state of dependence and protection. Being frightened by the deep insecurity of life, and shrinking from facing the world with all its disappointments and hardships, man sets up a religious system, says Freud, by which he can revert to the protection which a child enjoys from its father. The dogmas of the religious system which make possible belief in intelligence, purpose, and moral law in the universe "are illusions, fulfillments of the oldest, strongest and most insistent wishes of mankind." [1] Religion appeals to man's neurotic tendencies; in fact, "religion would be the universal obsessional neurosis of humanity." [2] Freud concludes by prophesying that with the advancement of the human race and the progress of science, religion will gradually be abandoned.

It must be admitted that there is an element of truth in all this. For some people *do* use religion as a means of buttressing themselves in a half-way state of development, a method by which they construct for themselves a nest of false security and protection from which they can view life as a sweet and rosy affair. But as a matter of fact, all aspects of culture can be used this way when seized upon by the neurotic individual. Literature can be a flight from life, abetting ill health; but it can also be a most efficacious exercise in the promotion of psychological adjustment. The same with philosophy and art, and even science. [3] Interestingly enough, science is the most flagrant example of man's endeavor to compensate for his basic insecurity; the frightened individual, overwhelmed by life's unpredictability, often flees to the scientific laboratory and there through analysis gains a certain mastery over the forces of life and feels himself to be in a protected haven.

This *abuse* of religion is what Freud is attacking. And to that extent he is right, and has much of value to teach us. But true religion, namely a fundamental affirmation of the meaning of life, is something without which no human being can be healthy in personality.

## THE NEED FOR MEANING

WHAT, in the last analysis, is wrong with the neurotic? We have described his malady from many points of view in these pages: maladjustment of tensions, fighting against himself, inability to make connections with his fellow men, and so on. All of these explanations are correct as far as they go. But can we now pierce deeper and discover a basic source of the neurosis underneath these various expressions?

It is agreed that the neurotic's problem at bottom is one of attitude. This attitude can best be described as an inability to *affirm*. "Affirm" means more than merely "accept"; it is rather accepting actively, saying "yes" not only verbally or mentally but as a response of one's total personality. The neurotic cannot affirm himself—and therefore he is at war with himself, a state which brings about the disunity we have often mentioned. He cannot affirm his situation among his fellow men—and so he regards them with suspicion and hostility. And finally, the neurotic cannot affirm life as a whole; he cannot affirm the universe—he feels it, too, is his enemy. This sounds illogical, but the neurotic's attitudes are based upon illogic. He has been hurled from his mother's womb against his wishes, he seems to be telling us; and, if we may judge from his actions, he is desirous of going back into the womb again.

This lack of ability to affirm himself, his fellow men, and the universe, is connected with the neurotic's accentuated feeling of insecurity. Everyone feels insecure to some extent, as we have said; it is part of the price we pay for living as individuals. But the neurotic, differing from the healthy person, cannot make terms with this insecurity; it frightens him too much; it paralyzes his action and throws his personality into panic.

Inability to affirm is merely another term for inability to *trust*. Not being able to trust, the neurotic lacks *confidence* and the related quality, *courage*. He must therefore endeavor to remain dependent in some situation of false security.

These qualities are linked together: if the neurotic had the power to trust, and collaterally confidence and courage, he could give an affirmative answer to life. And giving this affirmative answer, he would in a measure affirm his insecurity, and be fitted then to overcome it constructively. Because of his inability to affirm, he is caught in a vicious circle, which we saw led ultimately to his nervous breakdown. And so, finally, his life is to be described as *lacking in meaning*. He cannot *believe* in himself or in others or in the universe.

Now this is clearly a religious problem. For if the neurotic could *trust*, in the religious sense, could believe in himself and others, could have confidence that the universe has meaning in which his own insecurity can be overcome, then he could obtain the confidence and courage which he needs to live. As Jung well expresses it: "Among all my patients in the second half of life—that is to say, over thirty-five—there has not been one whose problem in the last resort was not that of finding a religious outlook on life. It is safe to say that every one of them fell ill because he had lost that which the living religions of every age have given to their followers, and none of them has been really healed who did not regain his religious outlook." [4] This holds, broadly speaking, for persons in the first half of life as well. It is the problem of the individual's finding meaning in his own life and ultimate meaning in the life-process. What he needs to live, says Jung, is "faith, hope, love, and insight." [5]

To approach the question from the negative side, let

us ask what happens to mental health when this meaning which religion gives is absent? In other words, what is the effect of atheism on personality? Here we find some very interesting data.

Frank R. was a real atheist. At the time of this interview, he was a sophomore in college, an intellectually brilliant young man from a cultural background. But he was not getting on well in college. He was studying practically none at all and hence was in academic difficulties in spite of his high intelligence. He was not looking forward to any particular vocation; in fact, he seemed to have no engrossing interests. He spent his time reading widely but superficially, getting drunk, and leading a reckless sort of social life. Indeed, he was continually in such an oppressive state of melancholy that drinking and using women as his playthings were his only means of relief. He was of course cynical; he rarely smiled when he talked to me, and in general he was very unhappy. His home background had been neutral in the respect of religion, and he claimed himself an atheist.

Most students who call themselves atheists actually are not; but there is no doubt in the matter of Frank R.'s being an atheist. The proof of the matter is that there was no meaning of any sort, practically speaking, in his life. His personality was disintegrating; he was, as we should expect, bristling with problems. He felt no purpose in his living. And from the health point of view, he was clearly neurotic.

I have been startled by the fact that practically every genuine atheist with whom I have dealt has exhibited unmistakable neurotic tendencies. How account for this curious fact? Is it merely that we tend to classify atheists as neurotics because they are, by definition, in rebellion against one aspect of accepted culture? There is a deeper reason than that. We observe that the distinguishing characteristic of Frank R. was his lack of purpose. Of course his personality was disintegrating, for there was no core. It was more in this case than a question of maladjustment of tensions—there was a lack of pattern around which the adjustment could be made. This is why a denial of purpose, either in his own life or in life as a whole, is so serious for the neurotic. He has no style of life, so to speak, for his life is not moving in any direction. Consequently Frank R. could find no meaning in his existence. Life was to him indeed a

> "tale
> Told by an idiot, full of sound and fury,
> Signifying nothing."

This is the state of neurosis which can be described by the religious term "hell"; the gradual disintegration, the breakdown in unity, the fighting of one's self and everything else, is certainly a hell if ever such existed.

The individual must have some belief in purpose in his life, however fragmentary, if he is to achieve personality health. Without purpose there cannot be meaning; and without meaning one cannot, in the end, live. Purpose serves in personality like a steel core in an electro-magnet —it unifies the lines of force and thus enables the magnet to exert effective power.

Personality health also requires that the individual believe in some purpose in the total life-process as well as in his own life. For one cannot live on an island of meaning surrounded by an ocean of meaninglessness. If the universe is crazy, the parts of it must be crazy too. This supports the original statement above, that the neurotic needs to affirm himself and society and the universe all at once; the three aspects of affirmation of life go together.

This is precisely what religion consists of. For religion is the belief in purpose, and therefore meaning, in the total life-process. Not of course the religion of a Harold K. or of any dogmatic sect, but religion as a basic attitude as man confronts his existence. Therefore, it is a fundamental truth that religion, with its faith in purpose, intelligence, and moral order in the universe, furnishes the indispensable undergirding for personality health.

Jung finds the needed meaning in the deepest levels of the collective unconscious. Here is the source of religion and of God, for the idea of God is an archetype, a "primordial image." The "idea of an all-powerful divine being is present everywhere, if not consciously recognized, then unconsciously accepted, because it is an archetype. .... Therefore I consider it wiser to recognize the idea of God consciously; otherwise something else becomes god, as a rule something quite inappropriate and stupid." [6] In the healing process of the neurotic, says Jung, "the archetypes come to independent life and serve as spiritual guides for the personality, thus supplanting the inadequate ego with its futile willing and striving. As the religious-minded person would say: guidance has come from God. .... I must express myself in more modest terms and say that the psyche has awakened to spontaneous life." [7] Finding religion consists of finding these deep levels of the unconscious and assimilating them into one's conscious living. Jung describes people who achieve that: "They came to themselves, they could accept themselves, they were able to become reconciled to themselves, and by this they were also reconciled to adverse circumstances and events. This is much like what was formerly expressed by saying: He has made his peace with God, he has sacrificed his own will, he has submitted himself to the will of God." [8]

Defining God as an archetype sounds strange to modern ears, but it has good theological support in history. It is similar to Plato's Idea of the Good, the ultimate idea or archetype which he calls God. Christian mystics have often talked of finding God in the deepest stratum of the self (what Jung calls the collective unconscious), where subjectivity and objectivity are overcome; "in the depths of the soul," said Augustine, "thought and being are one."

Jung's explanation of religious experience is stimulating and helpful, but it is incomplete. It emphasizes God's immanence in the individual, but its danger is in stopping here and identifying God with the deep levels in the self. In other words, is God only your unconscious self, or, what is not very different from a qualitative point of view, the collective selves of a group of people? Jung's view requires balance by an emphasis on the transcendent nature of God, which is found in Christian theology.

### PSYCHOTHERAPY NEEDS THEOLOGY

THE DEEPER one's thought penetrates in the field of psychotherapy, the closer one comes to the realm of theology. Psychotherapy begins with the problem of how the neurotic individual is to live most effectively; this becomes the problem of finding meaning in the neurotic's life, and at this point psychotherapy finds itself dealing with theological subjects. The fundamental questions with which psychotherapy ends can be answered only in the field of theology.

We found this true in our original analysis of personality in the second chapter. There it was discovered (it will be helpful for the reader to review the concluding section of that chapter) that any adequate picture of personality must take into consideration the tension in man's nature between what he is and what he ought to be—or better expressed, the contradiction between egocentric-

ity (man's selfish motives in his decisions) and social interest (responding unselfishly to the needs of others). This
is stated theologically as the contradiction between sin in
man's nature and response to the universal structure, or
God. It will be remembered that the psychotherapists
Jung, Rank, and Kunkel frankly recognized this contradiction, which they termed the "dualism" in human nature, and explicitly admitted their dependence on theology
for answers in this most important area.

The answer given by Christian theology, as indicated
in the preceeding chapter, is that man has a relationship to
God. This is so fundamental in man that it is attributed
to his creation, where he was "made in the image of God."
But man has freedom to live his own life, to make his own
moral decisions; he was given autonomy, and hence he has
self-will, and tends always to makes decisions according to
his own egocentricity rather than being true to the image
of God within him. So the image of God is always a
goal, a potentiality, but no man "arrives" at it or achieves
it. This means that there is always within man a tension
between God and man's egocentric will. This tension
makes life difficult; it results in our continual moral conflicts, our inner torments, and our guilt feelings. But the
tension is inescapable if personality is to have any meaning,
if freedom and moral autonomy, responsibility and salvation, are to have any meaning. In short, our reward for
bearing this tension is creativity in personality.

Man would indeed find himself in an impossible situation, were it not for "grace." This is a theological term,
but it has its corresponding term in psychotherapy, "clarification." When the neurotic individual is caught in the
vicious circle of egocentricity, and he cannot adequately
bear the tension which his freedom lays upon him and so
misuses his autonomy in self-defeating egocentricity, he is

enabled by "clarification" to break the throttling clutch of egocentricity. Then he is able to respond to the demands of the universe, as Kunkel says, or in our terms, respond to the call of God. What happens psychologically we can describe as follows: the neurotic individual has finally suffered so much from his vicious circle of egocentricity that he is willing to give up. He is willing to give up anything, his life if need be. He is in that state in which he is able to say, "Not my will but thine be done." He is in a position to respond. At that moment he feels he is not significant as a self-willing creature, but significant only because he can be to some small extent the channel of the meaning of the universe. Fortunately the structure of the universe (from the religious point of view, God), has been there all the time with its call; and when the individual is able to respond he is able to act without a predominantly egocentric motive. Because he has lost his life he has saved it. He has become "clarified."

We are right in calling this the *grace of God*, for it is preposterous to think that the individual does it for himself. He gives up; and the healing force of the universe, if one wishes to term it that, comes to his rescue. It is not that the person deserves it; only when he gets over thinking he deserves it is he in a position to receive help.

Then the individual will have gained a feeling of his own minuteness and insignificance in the face of the greatness of the universe and God's purposes therein. Thus he will experience what some persons like to call a "cosmic humility." This relieves him of his burden of arrogance. But his "insignificance" actually refers only to his egocentricity; he senses even more than previously his own important worth in the respect that as a personality he participates in the divine logos of meaning and can understand flashes of it now and then. He will take the attitude of "giving back" to the universe some of the debt he as a creature owes—and this is the root of a valid feeling of *duty*. He will recognize that there are purposes which swing in arcs much greater than his little orb, and he will aim to put himself in harmony with them. He will realize, without sentimentality, his dependence on God.

This clarification, or experience of grace, does not happen all at once and once and for all, so that thereafter the individual can proceed with never a care. No, those who think that being "saved" releases them permanently from the fundamental tension have missed the point altogether, and have fallen into a slough of false "sanctification" which is even more subtly egocentric. The clarified individual feels his guilt, as we stated earlier, with even greater sensitivity.

It is, rather, a new adjustment of tensions in the personality, and an adjustment that must continually be remade. There is a peak experience, a "conversion": after the climax of suffering and the sudden influx of understanding, the adjustment of tensions becomes easier. One is better able to continue tuning himself to respond without egocentricity. But the grace must be a continuous gift, just as clarification is.

It is important to remember that the clarified individual still has the "old Adam" within him, but he is able to confront this egocentric tendency successfully. He is not suddenly removed to a blissful state; but he is able to meet his divided state with an ultimate assurance of victory. The tension remains, but clarification (here we use the term as synonymous with grace) has removed the poison from the fangs of egocentricity. The person still tends to make selfish decisions; but through his awareness of the tendency, and through his realization that God's grace is continuously available, he is able continuously to "give up";

and thus his living is that much the less egocentric in motivation.

This "giving up" does not at all mean that the individual renounces some of his creativity, thereby tending to become static and unproductive. On the contrary, the achievement of grace and clarification of which we are speaking effects precisely the most creative adjustment of tensions within the individual. His egocentricity has been the blockage to his creativity. And freed from that he is able to express his creativity much more directly, spontaneously, and gratifyingly. In the words of Paul, the fetters of the law have been removed, and the spirit is able to rise up on its own wings. There is a creativity of grace. And in this the individual does not waste his energies struggling against inhibitions, constrictions, and other hindrances which his egocentricity places in the way. The freed energies of the artist, no longer absorbed in wrestling with himself, can woo beauty directly.

Man is still guilty; clarification and grace do not wipe the guilt away. But one is enabled to accept and affirm the guilt. The very accepting of it, the realization of it—which is classically termed "repentance"—is connected with the coming of grace. The fact that guilt, or sin, or egocentricity, or whatever one may term it, is never completely wiped away proves the importance of humility in the experience. There is no, "Lord, I thank thee that I am not as other men." Presumptuous satisfaction in one's own salvation is out of place both psychologically and religiously. Psychologically this is so because the more clarified one becomes, the more one realizes one's imperfect condition in personality. And religiously it is so because the more one receives the grace of God, the more one realizes one's guilt, and therefore the more one needs God's grace. The paradox is understandable that the man who is most sensitive to

God's grace should, in fact *must*, call himself the "chief of sinners."

Some people accept and affirm only what is good in themselves, or affirm the universe only so long as it is good to them. This is an error into which our utopian tendencies lead us, and it misses the deep aspects of the matter. It is as though one would affirm only a blissful world, about which one could sing, "God's in his heaven, all's right with the world." If all were right with the world, there would be no meaning in personality, and certainly no need for religion. Ultimately things may be right, but that is God's business. In man's particular situation all is not right: there is disharmony within himself, and there is disharmony in this diseased world. Psychologically and religiously, illness follows from any attempt to escape this disharmony. It is the pampered child who is willing to "play" only so long as the universe plays his way. The healthy individual, on the other hand, becomes willing to walk the knife-blade edge of insecurity and to affirm truth and goodness even though truth is on the scaffold and goodness is never perfectly achieved. Job teaches us much here; namely, the necessity of affirming goodness even though the individual himself tastes little of it. The reward of mental and religious health will come to him who is able to cry with Job, "Though He slay me, yet will I trust Him."

A unique sense of freedom surges in upon one after the experience of clarification and grace. Released from the unbearable conflict within himself, a man is free to choose rightly. His bondage to egocentricity and sin is in an important respect broken, and he can with Paul cry ecstatically of his new liberation.

The transformation from neurosis to personality health is indeed a wonderful process. The person rises on the force of hope out of the depths of his despair. His cowardice is replaced by courage. The rigid bonds of his selfishness are broken down by a taste of the gratification of unselfishness. Joy wells up and streams over his pain. And love comes into the man's life to vanquish his loneliness. He has at last found himself—and found his fellow men and his place in the universe. Such is the transformation from neurosis to personality health. And such is what it means, likewise, to experience religion.

# APPENDIX

# REFERENCES AND NOTES

## CHAPTER II

1. "Psychotherapy," a term which will be used often in this book, is compounded of "psycho" and "therapy," and means a curing by psychological means. Psychoanalysis is merely one form, the Freudian form, of psychotherapy. Counseling has definite relations to psychotherapy, as explained elsewhere in our discussion.

2. A very brief *historical sketch* of the development of psychotherapy may be apropos here. This includes several of the great historical philosophers who made special contributions to our understanding of personality.

   Its roots are to be seen far back in Socrates' philosophy, illustrated in such maxims as, "Know thyself," and, "Knowledge is virtue," which re-appear particularly in modern Adlerian thought. Plato exhibits profound insights on love and the nature of the unconscious which have their modern counterparts, especially in Jungianism. Ancient Stoicism made great endeavors to subject psychological processes to rational control; *vide* Marcus Aurelius' *Meditations.* We do not have space to indicate the importance of such early philosophies as Epicureanism, or early Christian mysticism. But Augustine should be mentioned as one of the most profound of early psychologists; his idea that in the depths of the individual soul the cleavage between subjectivity and objectivity is overcome is a classic statement still valid as the central presupposition of psychotherapy.

   Descartes (seventeenth century) set the problem which psychotherapy aims to solve in his unfortunate separation of mind from bodily functions. Then Spinoza endeavored to set up a scheme of psychological control of one's self by very rationalistic means. His ideas that the quality of our happiness depends on the things we love, that the things we fear are harmful only in our minds, that every passion is a confused idea and can be clarified by calm understanding, show a psychological understanding which is penetrating even if incomplete (see his *Ethics*).

Rousseau (eighteenth century) is exceedingly important as one of the chief figures in the romantic movement upon which modern psychotherapy depends. In his living, thinking, and preaching, Rousseau embodied the emotionalism, the rebellion against the restraints of society, and the "back to nature" cravings which romantics have always felt, and which take a prominent place in modern psychotherapeutic thought (*cf.* Freud's *Civilization and Its Discontents*). These aspects of Rousseau's thought are basic in later psychotherapy: vitalism (or emphasis on life force), reaction against rationalism, individualism, confidence in nature. He believed in self-expression, living one's self out to the full. His definition of education as a "direct and unconscious unfolding of the individual" (*Emile*) has surprising affinities with the Adlerian view. His confidence in the goodness of human nature also comes out in Adlerian thought.

Schopenhauer and Nietzsche (nineteenth century) are important precursors of psychotherapy, the former in his development of the "will and idea" problem, and the latter in his amazingly astute psychological insights. Nietzsche was a psychoanalyst who in many ways predicted later trends. He sensed something of the meaning of dreams. His introspection disclosed to him many truths regarding the function of the unconscious; he realized that the conclusions of the philosophers were actually pictures of their own deep selves, and that external problems were only stepping stones to the central area, namely self-knowledge. He saw that inner conflicts can be "sublimated" into art

**or** striving for power. His idea that "instinct is the most intelligent of all kinds of intelligence" (*Beyond Good and Evil*, p. 162) has curiously close parallels in statements of Jung. His concept of "will to power" has resemblance to Adler's central idea of the universal striving for power; but in reality Nietzsche is more Freudian. The negative view of society, the excessive laudation of individual strength, and the idea that all moral categories should be transcended in the end, are concepts which Nietzsche and Freud hold in common. They both see that instinctual expression leads in the end to destruction; but Nietzsche makes of this a tragic life-view, whereas Freud ends in pessimism.

The development of science in the nineteenth century also had an important influence on psychotherapy. Here Freud obtained his devotion to the scientific method and his belief that it is possible to bring human emotions and mind under control by analysis just as science brings the natural order under its control.

In the development of modern psychotherapy itself, Sigmund Freud, in his work beginning the last of the nineteenth century, is unchallengably the pioneer. Jung and Adler, originally associated with Freud, broke from him to establish their own schools in the early years of this century. Jung terms his branch "Analytic Psychology," and Adler his "Individual Psychology," to distinguish them from Freud's "Psychoanalysis." Rank deviated from the Freudian school only a few years ago. Fritz Kunkel began as an Adlerian and developed certain unique contributions of his own.

Thus, in the roots of modern psychotherapy, we find the thought streams of *romanticism, rationalism,* and *science* all important. In general psychotherapy can be designated as romantic in its metaphysical presuppositions, rationalistic in many of its practices (particularly Adlerianism), and scientific in its general technique (especially Freudianism).

3. Freud has written a great number of works dealing with various aspects of his system, and there are available innumerable semi-authoritative expositions by members of the Freudian school. To recommend a single book, however, we should cite as the most useful the recent *New Introductory Lectures on Psychoanalysis*, which presents the central Freudian theses in their more profound and developed form.

4. *A General Introduction to Psychoanalysis*, p. 375.

5. "There is nothing undetermined in the psychic life." *The Psychopathology of Everyday Life*, p. 282.

6. "Psychoanalysis extends the region of science to the mind of mankind." *New Introductory Lectures on Psychoanalysis*, p. 218. In this section Freud holds that science is the only admissible form of human knowledge, and in the final chapter in this book he explains his devotion to science as the hope of mankind. Freud's overvaluation of the scientific method and human reason are to be seen in such statements as, "It would be an illusion to suppose that we could get anywhere else what it (science) cannot give us" (*Future of an Illusion*, p. 98), and, "There is no appeal beyond reason" (*ibid.*, p. 49). For a discussion of the true function of science, and an explanation of the general failure to recognize the limits of science, of which Freudianism is an example, see Whitehead's *The Function of Reason*.

Rank's criticism is to the point: "The psychoanalytic striving to educate the individual exclusively in natural science, casual thinking, which Freud advocates in his last writing (*Der Zukunft einer Illusion*, 1927) is fortunately not possible, but betrays his whole moralistic pedagogical attitude, the very opposite of the attitude necessary for a constructive therapy of the individual." *Will Therapy*, p. 62.

7. I am indebted to Professor Paul Tillich for this viewpoint.

8. Otto Rank's recent books, *Will Therapy* and *Truth and Reality*, give stimulating and profound discussions of the

function of will in personality and the importance of such qualities as freedom, personal autonomy, and moral responsibility.

9. The central importance of creative will in Rank's view of personality is indicated in such statements as, "the creative type is able to create voluntarily from the impulsive elements and moreover to develop his standards beyond identifications of the super-ego morality to an ideal formation which consciously guides and rules this creative will in terms of personality. The essential point in this process is the fact that he evolves his ego ideal from himself, not merely on the ground of given but also of self-chosen factors which he strives after consciously." *Truth and Reality*, p. 9.

   Rank explains that this conception of creative, personal autonomy "makes creative power and creative accomplishment comprehensible for the first time, rather than the insipid and impotent concept of sublimation, which prolongs a shadowy existence in psychoanalysis." *Ibid.*, p. 11.

10. Another aspect of Rank's thought is especially significant for us, namely, his idea that the neurotic is the "artiste manque," the artist, that is, who cannot produce any art. The neurotic is the individual who desires to create—in fact, is forced to create, which in the long last is all anyone is forced to do in life—but for some reason cannot produce any creative work. Thus the neurotic, or for that matter any individual with a pronounced personality difficulty, may well be precisely the individual who possesses unusual creative potentialities, but is unable to adjust the tensions within his personality so as to bring these powers into effective expression. "I attempt to show in the neurotic," says Rank, "the superhuman, divine spark." *Will Therapy*, p. 141.

11. *Truth and Reality*, p. 66.

12. *Ibid.*, p. 40. Also: "In my view the patient should make himself what he is, should will it and do it himself, without

force or justification and without need to shift the responsibility for it." *Ibid.*, p. 41.

13. "If a man so thinks, feels, and acts, in a word so lives, as to correspond directly with objective conditions and their claims, whether in a good sense or ill, he is extroverted." *Psychological Types*, p. 417.

14. *Modern Man in Search of a Soul*, p. 69.

15. *Ibid.*, p. 69. Jung's broad emphasis upon the force and influence of unconscious and irrational factors in living is illustrated in such statements as, "The unconscious is capable at times of assuming an intelligence and purposiveness which are superior to actual conscious insight" (*Psychology and Religion*, p. 45), and, "In human affairs what appears impossible upon the way of the intellect has very often become true upon the way of the irrational. Indeed, all the greatest changes that have ever affected mankind have come not by the way of intellectual calculation, but by ways which contemporary minds either ignored or rejected as absurd, and which only long afterwards became fully recognized through their intrinsic necessity" (*Psychological Types*, p. 113). Consequently Jung places great value upon phantasy: "But what great thing ever came into existence that was not first phantasy?" (*Ibid.*, p. 77.) "It is not the artist alone, but every creative individual whatsoever who owes all that is greatest in his life to phantasy. The dynamic principle of phantasy is 'play,' which belongs also to the child, and as such it appears to be inconsistent with the principle of serious work. But without this playing with phantasy no creative work has ever yet come to birth." (*Ibid.*, p. 82.)

16. *Modern Man in Search of a Soul*, p. 190.

17. Jung states that his "archetypes" are identical with the Platonic "ideas." The archetypes, he says, are like "ideas born in one's blood." (Quoted from a lecture.)

18. "Artistic disposition involves an overweight of collective psychic life as against the personal. Art is a kind of innate drive that seizes a human being and makes him its instru-

ment. . . . . The artist . . . . is 'man' in a higher sense—he is 'collective man'—one who carries and shapes the unconscious, psychic life of mankind." (*Modern Man in Search of a Soul*, p. 195.) "Whenever the creative force predominates, human life is ruled and moulded by the unconscious as against the active will, and the conscious ego is swept along on a subterranean current, being nothing more than a helpless observer of events." (*Ibid.*, p. 197.) "The secret of artistic creation and of the effectiveness of art is to be found in a return to the state of *participation mystique*—to that level of experience at which it is man who lives, and not the individual, and at which the weal or woe of the single human being does not count, but only human existence." (*Ibid.*, p. 198, 199.)

19. It may be interesting to pass on some impressions of Dr. Adler the man, with whom I have had the prized privilege of studying, associating, and conversing intimately. Dr. Adler was the kind of person the French term "sympatique"; to talk with him was to have that rare privilege of a human relationship without barriers. One of his chief characteristics was his ability to remain relaxed, even in discussion; it was impossible to feel tense in his company. The criticism of superficiality that is leveled against some of his ideas is to an extent justified, but it is none the less true that his system as a whole will go down in history as a lasting contribution to the endeavor of man to understand himself.

20. Adler describes the ego as having much more power as a directing agent than the Freudian ego.

One of the chief differences between the Adlerian and Freudian systems is in the respect that Adler emphasizes the present *purpose* of the individual rather than the determining factors in his background. His system is teleological rather than causological. Whereas Freud deals chiefly with the causative factors in the individual's past, such as childhood experiences, Adler concerns himself with the direction in which the individual is moving.

21. Probably the most useful single book of Adler's is the readable *Understanding Human Nature*.

22. *What Life Should Mean to You.*

23. Jung is very outspoken on this point: "But individuation means precisely a better and more complete fulfilment of the collective dispositions of mankind, since an adequate consideration of the peculiarity of the individual is more conducive to a better social achievement, than when the peculiarity is neglected or repressed." (*Two Essays in Analytical Psychology*, p. 184.)

24. Freud says in one place that guilt feeling is an expression of the tension between the ego and the super-ego (*New Introductory Lectures on Psychoanalysis*, p. 88), and in another that it represents a masochistic tendency toward self punishment. But Freud does not understand the nature of the normal guilt feeling of which we are speaking, as he does not understand the role of freedom, autonomy, and responsibility in personality. His naturalism confines him to the existential level; and hence no genuine guilt feeling, such as leads to religious tension, is admissible. As Rank says, "In Psychoanalytic theory . . . . *guilt feeling is and remains a final insoluble fact*" (*Truth and Reality*, p. 32.)

25. This is what Thomas Mann has in mind when he quotes Degas as saying, "A picture must be painted with the same feeling as that with which a criminal commits his crime." Then Mann adds, "This is the precious and guilty secret," as he refers to Goethe's refusal to talk about his creative projects when he was in the process of producing them. (*Freud, Goethe and Wagner*, p. 85.)

26. *Truth and Reality*, p. 62. The quotation continues, ". . . . and even if there were none of the numerous proofs for the inner freedom of conscious will, the fact of human consciousness of guilt alone would be sufficient to prove the freedom of the will as we understand it psychologically beyond a doubt." And, "In a word, will and guilt are the

two complementary sides of one and the same phenomenon." (*Ibid.* p. 62.)

27. This has been spoken of historically as the "dualism" in man's nature. To indicate that we are still on good psychological ground, let us quote Rank and Jung on the matter. "Man suffers from a fundamental dualism, however one may formulate it, and not from a conflict created by forces in the environment which might be avoided by a 'correct bringing up' or removed by later re-education (psychoanalysis)." (*Will Therapy,* p. 173.) Jung speaks of it in the terms of St. Paul, "old Adam" and the "new man." Each extreme is "salvaging only a narrow state of consciousness. The alternative is to shatter it with the tension inherent in the play of opposites—in the dualistic stage—and thereby to build up a state of wider and higher consciousness." (*Modern Man in Search of a Soul,* p. 117.) Putting on the "new man" does not mean getting rid of the "old Adam." Being aware of one's divided state is the third and highest step in consciousness.

## CHAPTER III

1. *Psychological Types,* p. 368. Also, "But since the feeling-into subject feels his activity, his life, into the object, he therewith also yields himself to the object."

2. *Understanding Human Nature,* pp. 60, 61.

3. *Modern Man in Search of a Soul,* p. 57. Jung also says here: "We cannot by any device bring it about that the treatment is not the outcome of a mutual influence in which the whole being of the patient as well as that of the doctor plays its part. Two primary factors come together in the treatment—that is, two persons, neither of whom is a fixed and determinable magnitude. . . . . You can exert no influence if you are not susceptible to influence. It is futile for the doctor to shield himself from the influence of the patient and to surround himself with a smoke-screen of fatherly and professional authority." (This whole book is to be recommended to every counselor.)

4. *How Natives Think*, p. 364. Other quotations from this important book pertain to our point: "Every individual *is* both such and such a man or woman, alive at present, a certain ancestral individual, who may be human or semi-human . . . . and at the same time he *is* his totem, that is, he partakes in mystic fashion of the essence of the animal or vegetable species whose name he bears. . . . . The verb 'to be' . . . . encompasses both the collective representation and the collective consciousness in a participation that is actually lived, in a kind of symbiosis effected by identity of essence." (*Ibid.*, p. 91.)

"Now the need of participation assuredly remains something more imperious and more intense, even among peoples like ourselves, than the thirst for knowledge and the desire for conformity with the claims of reason. It lies deeper within us and its source is more remote." (*Ibid.*, p. 385.)

5. *Ibid.*, p. 385.

6. It is not sentimentality, then, to speak of the power of faith to bring about a change in another individual. Faith in a person, be it the mother's in her child, or the young man's in his friend, or the wife's in her husband, actually does create a strong force for the strengthening or transforming of the other personality. This is an old religious truth which here receives psychological confirmation on the basis of our understanding of empathy.

7. See *New Frontiers of the Mind*, Farrar and Rinehart, 1937. Dr. Rhine's basic test concerned clairvoyance, a perceiving of a physical object without using any of the known senses. The technique consisted of the calling of symbols on specially prepared cards which the individual could not see, variants on this including tests from distances of a few feet to hundreds of miles, tests with the persons drugged or stimulated, etc. Dr. Rhine also made a great number of tests for pure telepathy. Certain of the persons taking the tests were able to hold an average distinctly above "chance," which was computed mathematically, for thou-

sands of tests. According to these experiments not every-one possesses the extra-sensory capacity in the same degree; Dr. Rhine's purpose was only to discover whether *some* persons possessed it.

8. *Ibid.*, p. 188.

9. *Ibid.*, p. 240.

10. *New Introductory Lectures*, pp. 78 ff. Freud believes that the balance of evidence at the moment is in favor of mental telepathy, and requests a more favorable attitude toward it. But he attempts, to my mind mistakenly, to interpret telepathy as a more complicated and subtle form of physical transference, like the telephone. There is no more reason for hypothesizing telepathy as sensory than as *extra*-sensory.

11. *Psychopathology of Everyday Life*, p. 255. Freud's explanation of his honesty follows: "As often as I attempt a distortion I succumb to an error or some other faulty act, which betrays my dishonesty." This proves our point, namely, that the psychologically rectified mind becomes more honest by dint of its own automatic processes.

12. Freud's explanation of the phenomenon of influence hinges on his theory of the super-ego, the parental function in the mind which sits in judgment, as it were, and endeavors to cajole the ego into paths decreed by society's morals, customs, and laws. But this Freudian super-ego plays only a minor role, and the role of a meddler at that. Its function is defined mostly as interference with the desired direct expression of the libido. Such a negative interpretation of influence we must regard as inadequate. This is just the point where the deterministic theories of personality break down most obviously, for a denial of creative will and a consequent over-emphasis on instinct make influence inexplicable.

13. The common practice of holding up Jesus as an ideal for youth is very much open to question. Serving Jesus and his cause is one thing; but trying to be another Jesus, or trying to assume his role in life as Savior, is a different

thing and carries very dangerous and hypocritical implications. Religious educators who advise youth in the latter direction have missed, it is fair to say, the meaning of Jesus' teaching and Christianity. He is the Son of God, the Savior in a way qualitatively different from that open to other men, and his value to us is far greater than that of an ethical example. The more sound approach in our religious education is to explain the goals advocated by Christianity, such as unselfish service and brotherly living, and to hold these up before youth. To the extent that the young person accepts these goals for himself, he will achieve empathy with the human element in Christ; and through this channel he will avail himself of the influence which is desired. Jung puts the matter poignantly: "It is no easy matter to live a life that is modelled on Christ's, but it is unspeakably harder to live one's own life as truly as Christ lived his. . . . . The modern man, moreover, is not eager to know in what way he can imitate Christ, but in what way he can live his own individual life, however meager and uninteresting it may be." (*Modern Man in Search of a Soul*, pp. 273, 274.)

14. "It is impossible," Adler points out, "to have a lasting influence upon an individual whom one is harming. One can influence another individual best when he is in the mood in which he feels his own rights guaranteed." (*Understanding Human Nature*, p. 63.)

15. *Modern Man in Search of a Soul*, p. 59.

## CHAPTER IV

1. Adler, *Understanding Human Nature*, p. 170.
2. I am using the term "character" to designate that external aspect of personality which is seen by the world.
3. Freud, *Psychopathology of Everyday Life*, p. 220.
4. Quoted by Adler, *Understanding Human Nature*, p. 252.
5. "We may deduce that all recollections have an unconscious purpose within themselves. They are not fortuitous

phenomena, but speak clearly the language of encouragement or of warning. . . . . We remember those events whose recollection is important for a specific psychic tendency, because these recollections further an important underlying movement." (*Ibid.*, pp. 48, 49.)

6. Adler's expression "style of life" means something very similar to our term "personality pattern," the chief difference being that "style of life" emphasizes the direction in which the individual is moving whereas "personality pattern" refers more to the adjustment of tensions within the individual which is the source of this movement.

7. Jones, an English psychoanalyst, says that the success of a psychotherapist can be judged by the number of personal belongings of his clients which accumulate in his office; for leaving something behind is an unconscious expression on the part of the patient of his desire to come back.

8. See Freud, *Psychopathology of Everyday Life*, and similar works by the other therapists.

9. See Chapter VIII in Adler's *Understanding Human Nature* for the best explanation of this subject.

## CHAPTER VII

1. *General Introduction to Psychoanalysis*, p. 374.

Adler likewise makes it clear that the decision must come from the patient: "The bringing about of a change in the nature of the patient can emanate from him alone. I always found it most profitable ostentatiously to sit with my hands in my lap, fully convinced the patient, no matter what I might be able to say on the point, as soon as he has recognized his life-line, can obtain nothing from me that he, as a sufferer, does not understand better." (*Practice and Theory of Individual Psychology*, p. 46.)

2. *Truth and Reality*, p. 41.

3. *Modern Man in Search of a Soul*, p. 260.

4. *Let's Be Normal*, p. 168.

5. Quoted by Elliott, *Solving Personal Problems*, p. 303.

## CHAPTER VIII

1. *The Problem of Lay Analyses*, p. 11.
2. It goes without saying that this use of religion as a cloak for one's own ego-striving is not the fault of the religion itself but rather of the neurotic tendencies of the individual in question, who assumes the religion. A true understanding of religion would get him over his neurosis, as we shall see in the final chapter.
3. In counseling with the type of person who endeavors to rule the specific sexual function out of his or her life, my question as to whether the counselee looks forward to marriage is often answered by, "Yes, I think it would be nice to have a home," or, "Yes, I want to have children." Now both having a home and children are essential aspects of marriage, but either or both motives as the main foundation of marriage are dangerous. We normally expect love for a member of the opposite sex to be the central motive leading to marriage, and when this is absent we may expect that the sex problem has not been satisfactorily handled. This general attitude toward marriage may carry over into the plan of isolating sexual relations to the once or twice a year when the conception of children is desired. There is no question psychologically that this is a harmful and dangerous practice.
4. *Understanding Human Nature*, p. 264.
5. *Ibid.*, p. 157.
6. *Modern Man in Search of a Soul*, p. 270.

## CHAPTER IX

1. *Understanding Human Nature*, p. 255.
2. Quoted from a letter of Rousseau by Hoffding, *Jean Jacques Rousseau and His Philosophy*, p. 76.
3. *Beyond Good and Evil*, p. 174.
4. Adler, *What Life Should Mean to You*, p. 262.

## CHAPTER X

1. Freud, *The Future of an Illusion*, p. 52.

2. *Ibid.*, p. 76. Freud attacks religion unsparingly in this and others of his books. But this is Freud at his least astute, and his polemics do him no credit. His discussion of religion shows a misunderstanding of what religion is, and he falls into a morass of inconsistencies.

3. Freud emphasizes the neurotic aspects of philosophy and art as well as religion, whereas Rank calls them "the great spontaneous therapies of man." *Truth and Reality*, p. 88.

4. *Modern Man in Search of a Soul*, p. 264.

5. *Ibid.*, p. 261.

6. *Two Essays on Analytical Psychology*, p. 73.

7. *Modern Man in Search of a Soul*, p. 279.

8. *Psychology and Religion*, p. 99.

Jung explains how this primordial image of God springs up in modern persons by describing the case of one of his patients who experienced the recurrent phantasy of being held in the arms of a very large man, appearing to her like a father. This large man was standing in a field with the wind blowing about. In such a phantasy, Jung points out, we have the image of the father, the idea of support and protection, and the blowing of the wind, which symbolizes the "spirit" character of the phantasy. In other words, this is the image of God springing up in the patient's mind. "We are dealing with a genuine and really primitive divine-image, which grew in the unconscious of a modern mind and produced a living effect, an effect which both in respect to religion and psychology might cause one to reflect." (*Two Essays on Analytical Psychology*, p. 138.)

Jung also holds that creeds and dogma are expressions of archetypes, representing the classic formulations of fundamental and universal truths. "A creed is always the result and fruit of many minds and many centuries, purified from all oddities, shortcomings, and flaws of individual experience." (*Psychology and Religion*, p. 63.)

Religious experience does not need rational proof or substantiation, Jung holds. "Religious experience is absolute. It is indisputable. . . . . No matter what the world thinks about religious experience, the one who has it possesses the great treasure of a thing that has provided him with a source of life, meaning, and beauty and that has given a new splendor to the world and to mankind." (*Ibid.*, p. 113.)

The healing of a neurosis is like a religious experience. "And if such experience helps to make your life healthier, more beautiful, more complete, and more satisfactory to yourself and to those you love, you may safely say: 'This was the grace of God.'" (*Ibid.*, p. 114.)

# BIBLIOGRAPHY

Adler, Alfred: *The Practice and Theory of Individual Psychology.* Translated by P. Radin. Harcourt, Brace and Co., New York, 1924.
  —*Understanding Human Nature.* Translated by Walter Beran Wolfe. Greenberg, New York, 1927.
  —*What Life Should Mean to You.* Edited by Alan Porter. Little, Brown and Co., Boston, 1931.
Elliott, H. S., and Elliott, G. L.: *Solving Personal Problems.* Henry Holt and Co., New York, 1937.
Freud, Sigmund: *The Future of an Illusion.* Translated by W. D. Robson-Scott. Horace Liveright, New York, 1928.
  —*A General Introduction to Psychoanalysis.* Authorized translation by G. Stanley Hall. Horace Liveright, New York, 1920.
  —*New Introductory Lectures on Psychoanalysis.* Translated by W. J. H. Sprott. W. W. Norton & Co., New York, 1933.
  —*The Problem of Lay-Analyses.* Translated by A. Paul Maerker-Brauden. Brentano's, New York, 1928.
  —*The Psychopathology of Everyday Life.* Authorized English edition, with introduction by A. A. Brill. Macmillan, New York, 1917.
Hoffding, H.: *Jean Jacques Rousseau and His Philosophy.* Translated by W. Richards and L. E. Saidla. Yale University Press, New Haven, 1930.
Jung, C. G.: *Modern Man in Search of a Soul.* Translated

by W. S. Dell and C. F. Baynes. Harcourt, Brace and Co., New York, 1933.

—*Psychology and Religion.* Yale University Press, New Haven, 1938.

—*Psychological Types; or, The Psychology of Individuation.* Translated by H. Godwin Baynes. Harcourt, Brace and Co., New York, 1923.

—*Two Essays in Analytical Psychology.* Translated by H. G. and C. F. Baynes. Dodd, Mead & Co., New York, 1928.

Kunkel, Fritz: *Let's Be Normal!* Translated by Eleanore Jensen. Ives Washburn, New York, 1929.

Levy-Bruhl, Lucien: *How Natives Think.* Authorized translation by Lilian A. Clare. George Allen & Unwin, London, 1926.

Mann, Thomas: *Freud, Goethe, Wagner.* Alfred A. Knopf, New York, 1937.

Nietzsche, Friedrich: *Beyond Good and Evil.* Translated by Helen Zimmern. London, 1909. The Modern Library, 1917.

Rank, Otto: *Truth and Reality.* Translated by Jessie Taft. Alfred A. Knopf, New York, 1936.

—*Will Therapy.* Translated by Jessie Taft. Alfred A. Knopf, New York, 1936.

Rhine, J. B.: *New Frontiers of the Mind.* Farrar and Rinehart, New York, 1937.

Whitehead, A. N.: *The Function of Reason.* Princeton University Press, Princeton, 1929.

# Index

## INDEX